THE PROFESSIONAL ARRANGER COMPOSER

RUSSELL GARCIA

14th PRINTING

CRITERION MUSIC CORPORATION

Exclusively Distributed By

7777 W. BLUEMOUND RD. P.O. BOX 13819 MILWAUKEE, WI 53213

FOREWORD

THE PURPOSES OF THIS BOOK ARE:
1) TO PROVIDE A TEXT-BOOK FOR THE MUSICIAN WHO WANTS TO BECOME A PROFESSIONAL ARRANGER-COMPOSER;

2) TO PROVIDE THE TEACHER AND THE SCHOOLS WITH A PRACTICAL TEXT;

3) TO OPEN UP AVENUES OF THINKING THAT POSSIBLY THE PROFESSIONAL DIDN'T REALIZE WERE THERE;

4) TO HELP IMPROVE MUSIC (AND THE TEACHING OF MUSIC) IN GENERAL;

5) TO PASS ON THE EXPERIENCE AND KNOWLEDGE OF THOUSANDS WHO HAVE GONE BEFORE, PLUS MY OWN EXPERIMENTATION, THAT OTHERS MAY TAKE AND PROGRESS A LITTLE FURTHER.

DO NOT BELIEVE ANYTHING YOU READ IN THIS BOOK UNTIL YOU HAVE WEIGHED IT OVER IN YOUR MIND AND TESTED IT IN ACTUAL PRACTICE.

I HAVE TRIED TO GIVE YOU GENERAL PRINCIPLES THAT I HONESTLY BELIEVE ARE TRUE TODAY. MUSIC AND PEOPLE ARE CONSTANTLY CHANGING, SO RULES THAT ARE TRUE NOW (TO THE BEST OF OUR KNOWLEDGE) WILL OF NECESSITY HAVE TO BE MODIFIED IN THE YEARS TO COME.

BEWARE OF THE MENTAL BLOCKS OR LIMITS PLACED ON YOUR THINKING BY ACCEPTING "IRON BOUND" RULES UNTHINKINGLY.
   IE: THE OLD THEORY BOOKS SAY THAT PARALLEL 5THS ARE FORBIDDEN. WE KNOW THAT THIS IS RIDICULOUS, AND IT MUST BE THROWN OUT OR MODIFIED TO FIT OUR PRESENT DAY THINKING. SO YOU CAN SEE THAT BLIND UNTHINKING BELIEF IN RULES CAN INHIBIT PROGRESS. WE MUST CONTINUALLY MODIFY THEM.

AN EFFORT WAS MADE TO PRESENT THIS BOOK IN EVERY DAY SIMPLE LANGUAGE, BUT MANY OF THE IDEAS REQUIRE AN OPEN MIND THAT IS WILLING TO ACCEPT NEW APPROACHES, AND IS WILLING TO PUT FORTH THE EFFORT TO ESTABLISH NEW HABITS OF THINKING THAT THEY MAY ADD TO THEIR OLD HABITS.
(SEE RHYTHMIC CURVES - EX.322-325)

MANY OF THE IDEAS THAT TAKE UP POSSIBLY ONE PAGE OF THE BOOK ARE THE RESULT OF YEARS OF EXPERIMENTING AND GROPING.

I HAVE BORROWED IDEAS FROM OTHER COMPOSERS AND WRITERS FOR THIS BOOK (WHERE IT WAS NECESSARY ONLY) TO SHOW HOW CERTAIN LEGITIMATE PRINCIPLES MAY BE APPLIED TO YOUR PRACTICAL WRITING.

ALSO, I WELCOME ANY DISCUSSION OF THE IDEAS SET FORTH HERE, BECAUSE THE MOTIVE THAT PROMPTED THIS BOOK WAS THE SEARCH FOR EASIER AND BETTER WAYS OF WRITING AND TEACHING AND PROGRESSING MUSIC.

NOTE: THIS IS THE SECOND PRINTING OF THIS HIGHLY SUCCESSFUL BOOK. WHEN CRITERION MUSIC CORPORATION ACQUIRED THE RIGHTS IN THIS PUBLICATION, MR. GARCIA SPECIFICALLY ASKED THAT WE RETAIN THE INFORMAL MECHANICAL CONSTRUCTION OF THE ORIGINAL FORMAT. HE FEELS THAT THIS INFORMALITY HAS A BENEFICIAL PSYCHOLOGICAL EFFECT UPON THE USER. THIS EDITION IS ALMOST IDENTICAL TO THE ORIGINAL PUBLICATION, WITH A FEW SLIGHT CHANGES INCLUDING REVISION OF THE PAGE NUMBERS.

ABOUT THE AUTHOR:

A TALENTED AND RESPECTED COMPOSER, "THE GUY WITH THE NICEST DISPOSITION" (AS HE IS KNOWN AROUND THE PICTURE STUDIOS); BORN IN OAKLAND, CALIFORNIA, AND NOW RESIDING WITH HIS FAMILY IN THE HOLLYWOOD HILLS.

ON STAFF AT N.B.C. (4 YEARS) AS COMPOSER-ARRANGER, NOW COMPOSER-CONDUCTOR FOR MANY MAJOR PICTURE STUDIOS. IN THE DANCE BAND FIELD, HE WRITES FOR SUCH BANDS AS BUDDY DE FRANCO, HARRY JAMES, ETC., (AND THERE'S HARDLY A NAME BAND IN THE COUNTRY THAT DOESN'T HAVE ONE OF HIS STUDENTS AS AN ARRANGER). HE IS ARRANGER FOR MANY TOP VOCALISTS AND RECORD COMPANIES AND HAS MANY NETWORK SHOWS TO HIS CREDIT. HE HAS FOUND TIME BETWEEN ASSIGNMENTS TO LECTURE AND TEACH HIS NEW AND PRACTICAL APPROACH AT MANY COLLEGES

IN OCTOBER, 1957, MR. GARCIA CONDUCTED THREE OF HIS OWN SYMPHONIC COMPOSITIONS IN THE STUTTGART MUSIC FESTIVAL IN GERMANY.

AMONG THE ARTISTS MR. GARCIA HAS RECORDED WITH ARE ELLA FITZGERALD, LOUIS ARMSTRONG, FRANCES FAYE, JULIE LONDON, OSCAR PETERSON, SARAH VAUGHN & INNUMERABLE OTHERS. ALBUMS OF HIS OWN ARE "FANTASTICA" & "HI-FI FOR KIDS-FROM 2 TO 92" (LIBERTY RECORDS), "LISTEN TO THE MUSIC OF RUSSELL GARCIA" (KAPP), "THE JOHNNY EVERGREENS" (ABC-PARAMOUNT), "SOUNDS IN THE NIGHT" & "FOUR HORNS & A LUSH LIFE" (BETHLEHEM).

MR. GARCIA HELD THE DISTINGUISHED OFFICE AS PRESIDENT OF THE BOHEMIAN CLUB OF LOS ANGELES, AND IS A MEMBER OF THE AMERICAN SOCIETY OF MUSIC ARRANGERS, THE COMPOSERS GUILD OF AMERICA, THE FRENCH HORN CLUB OF LOS ANGELES, ASCAP, AND LOCAL #47.

WE FEEL THAT MR. GARCIA HAS DONE A GREAT SERVICE TO THE FUTURE ARRANGER BY WRITING THIS CONCISE AND CLEAR BOOK.

THE EDITOR.

THE PROFESSIONAL ARRANGER COMPOSER

BY RUSSELL GARCIA

TABLE OF CONTENTS

RANGES & TRANSPOSITIONS 7

BOOK 1

DANCE BAND HARMONY & VOICING 16

    SCALES.. 16
    INTERVALS 17
    HOW TO BUILD CHORDS 19
    DANCE BAND CHORD SYMBOLS 19
    NON-CHORDAL NOTES 22
    TWO PART HARMONY 23
    THREE PART HARMONY 23
    FOUR PART TIGHT (BLOCK) HARMONY 25
    FOUR PART SPREAD (OPEN) HARMONY 28
    HARMONIZATION OF NON-CHORDAL NOTES 31
    FIVE PART HARMONY 33
    CLUSTERS 34
    BIG SPREAD CHORDS
      SIX, SEVEN & EIGHT PARTS 35
      VOICING BIG CHORDS 35
    ALTERING THE DOMINANT 7TH CHORD 37
    CONSONNANCE & DISSONANCE 42
    PRETTY NOTES AGAINST DIFFERENT TYPE CHORDS 43
    RESOLUTION OF BIG CHORDS 45
    SOLFEGGIO 46
    WRITING RHYTHMS 48

BOOK 11

FORM (PLANNING AN ARRANGEMENT) 53

    POSSIBILITIES OF DANCE BAND 54
    BACKGROUNDS 55
    PLANS FOR ARRANGEMENTS 62
    PIANO, BASS, GUITAR & DRUM PARTS 65

COUNTERPOINT IN DANCE BAND WRITING 66

© Copyright MCMLIV by CRITERION MUSIC CORP., 150 W. 55t   Y.
All Rights Reserved   International Copyright Secured   Printed in U.S.A.
THIRTEENTH PRINTING
BY ARRANGEMENT WITH BARRINGTON HOUSE PUBLISHERS

BOOK III

EXAMPLES OF PRESENT DAY DANCE BAND STYLES

- SMALL COMBO 73
- DIXIELAND 74
- TENOR BAND 76
- COMMERCIAL PIANO PARTS 77
- STOCK ORCHESTRATIONS & ARRANGEMENTS FOR ACTS 79
- VOCAL GROUPS 80
- DANCE BAND 54
- LARGER ORCHESTRAS 82
- STRINGS 84
- LATIN MUSIC 91

BOOK IV

INTROS, MODULATIONS, INTERLUDES & ENDINGS

- INTROS 105
- MODULATIONS 108
- ENDINGS 112
- EXTENSIONS 113

BOOK V

HARMONIC PROGRESSION

- ROOT PROGRESSION & CYCLES 116
- HARMONIC PROGRESSION FOR DIFFERENT STYLE SONGS .. 120
- ALTERED CHORDS 125
- SUBSTITUTE CHORDS 128
- MELODY WRITING 130
- FREEDOM OF EXPRESSION 134

BOOK VI

EXPERIMENTAL MATERIAL FOR THE PROGRESSIVE ARRANGER, COMPOSER

- PARALLEL OR SYMMETRIC HARMONY 139
- POLYTONALITY 140
- REFLECTIONS 141
- FREE CLUSTERS 142
- LINEAR HARMONY 142
- RHYTHMIC CURVES 143
- MASS MOTION 144
- OTHER SYSTEMS OF NOTATION 146
- BUILDING NEW SCALES & CHORDS 147
- COUPLINGS 148
- NON-CHORDAL NOTES 148
- ORGAN POINT 148
- WANDERING HARMONIES 149
- IMITATIONS 149
- DOUBLE & TRIPLE SEQUENCES 150
- TRICK CANNONS 151
- METHOD OF PROCEDURE FOR HARMONIZATION 152
- UNITY & VARIETY 155
- EXPLOITING A THEME OR MOTIVE 158
- ORCHESTRA SETUP 167

SUGGESTED COURSE OF STUDY FOR THE SERIOUS STUDENT .. 171

RANGES OF THE INSTRUMENTS

E♭ ALTO SAX:
(CONCERT RANGE)

TRANSPOSED RANGE
(UP A MAJOR SIXTH)

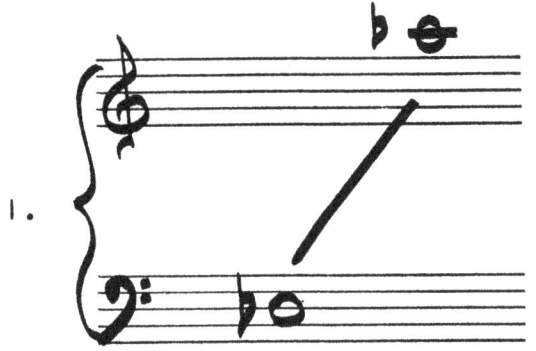
1.

2.

B♭ TENOR SAX:
(CONCERT RANGE)

TRANSPOSED RANGE
(UP A MAJOR NINTH)

3.

4.

E♭ BARITONE SAX:
(CONCERT RANGE)

TRANSPOSED RANGE
(UP AN OCTAVE AND A MAJOR SIXTH)

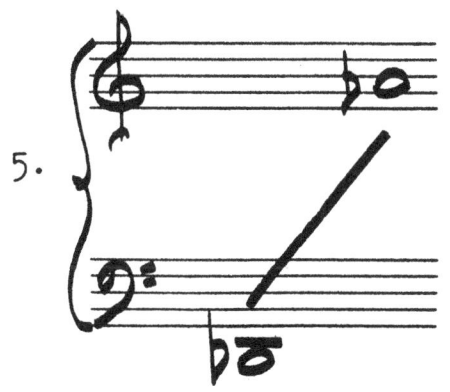
5.

6.

Bb CLARINET:
(CONCERT RANGE)

TRANSPOSED RANGE
(UP A MAJOR SECOND)

7.

8.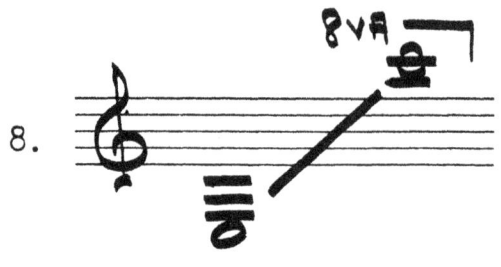

FLUTE:
(CONCERT RANGE)

NON-TRANSPOSING

9.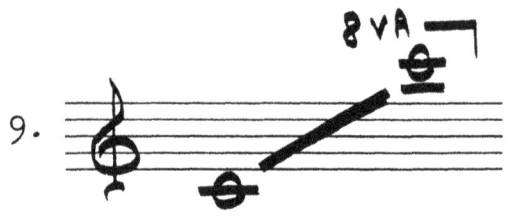

OBOE:

NON-TRANSPOSING

10.

ENGLISH HORN IN F:
(CONCERT RANGE)

TRANSPOSED RANGE
(UP A PERFECT FIFTH)

11.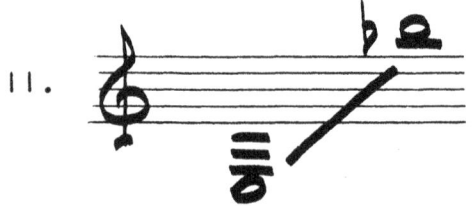

12.

BASSOON:

NON-TRANSPOSING

13.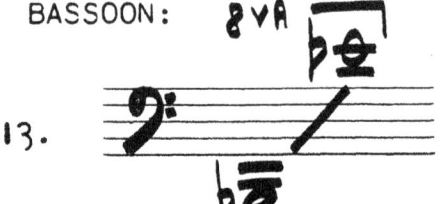

CONTRA BASSOON HAS THE SAME RANGE AS BASSOON BUT SOUNDS ONE OCTAVE LOWER THAN WRITTEN.

THE TOP THREE SEMITONES ON FLUTE, OBOE, ENGLISH HORN, CLARINET, AND BASSOON MUST BE USED WITH DISCRETION.

BASS CLARINET IS ONE OCTAVE LOWER THAN CLARINET SO IT MUST BE TRANSPOSED UP A MAJOR NINTH. IT IS MOST USEABLE IN THE LOW AND MEDIUM REGISTERS. MOST BASS CLARINETS NOW HAVE EXTRA KEYS WHICH ALLOW THEM TO PLAY A FEW SEMITONES BELOW THE NORMAL RANGE.

FRENCH HORN IN F:
 (CONCERT RANGE)

14.

TRANSPOSED RANGE
 (UP A PERFECT FIFTH)

15.

FOR FURTHER STUDY ON THE USAGE OF THESE INSTRUMENTS READ FORSYTHE "ORCHESTRATION."

B♭ TRUMPET:
 (CONCERT RANGE)

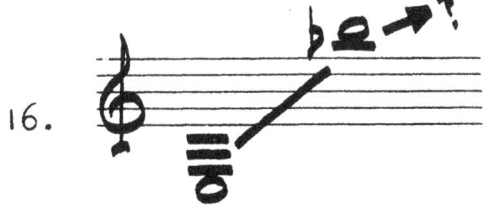

16.

TRANSPOSED RANGE
 (UP A MAJOR SECOND)

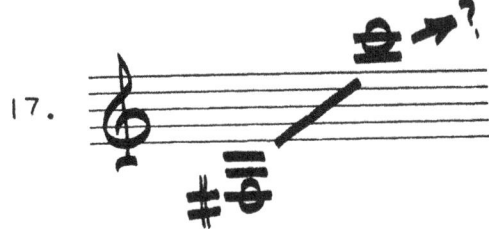

17.

TROMBONE:

18.

NON-TRANSPOSING

TUBA:

19.

NON-TRANSPOSING

VIOLIN:

20.

NON-TRANSPOSING

VIOLA:

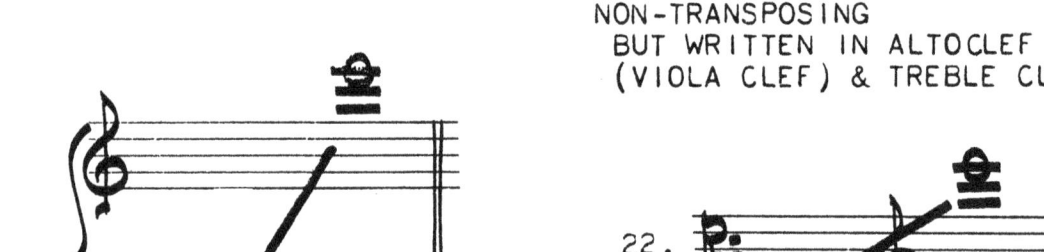

21.

NON-TRANSPOSING
BUT WRITTEN IN ALTO CLEF
(VIOLA CLEF) & TREBLE CLEF.

22.

CELLO:

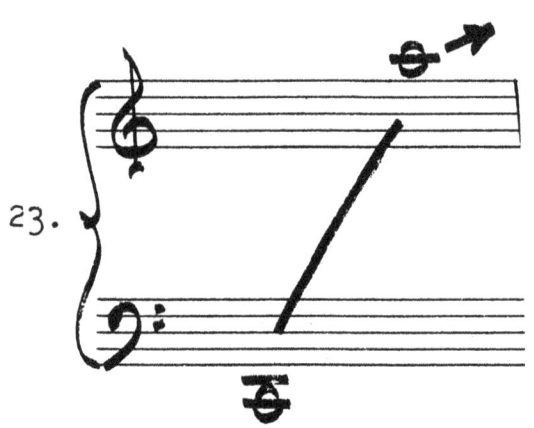

23.

NON-TRANSPOSING

STRING BASS:
(CONCERT RANGE)

24.

TRANSPOSED RANGE
SOUNDS ONE OCTAVE LOWER THAN WRITTEN

25.

GUITAR:
(CONCERT RANGE)

26.

TRANSPOSED RANGE
SOUNDS ONE OCTAVE LOWER THAN WRITTEN

27.

NON-TRANSPOSING

PIANO:

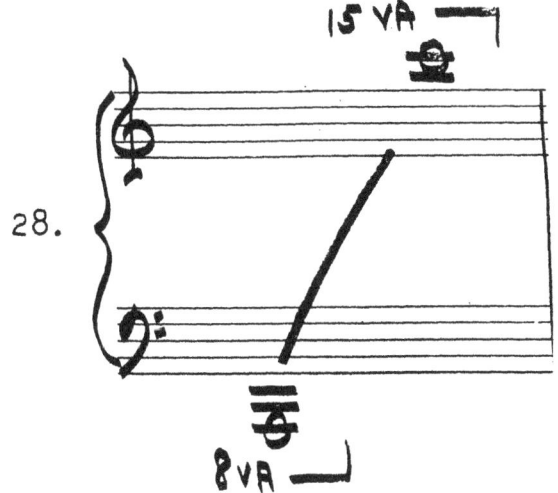

28.

LISTEN TO ORCHESTRAS ANALYTICALLY AND NOTICE WHAT TYPE OF MUSIC SOUNDS BEST AND MOST NATURAL FOR EACH INSTRUMENT.
   IE: BRASS SOUND BEST FOR PUNCHING AND ALSO ARE GOOD FOR BUILDING BIG CLIMAXES.
   SAXES ARE MORE ADEPT AT LEGATO ROLLING PASSAGES.

DON'T EXPECT STRINGS TO PHRASE LIKE BRASS OR SAXES BECAUSE THE TECHNIQUE OF BOWING IS MUCH DIFFERENT THAN THAT OF BLOWING.

ALWAYS LISTEN ANALYTICALLY!

WHAT ARE THE CONCERT RANGES OF:
   ALTO SAX, TENOR, BARITONE, TRUMPET, TROMBONE, STRING BASS?

TO SOUND CONCERT MIDDLE C, WHAT NOTE WOULD YOU WRITE FOR EACH OF THESE INSTRUMENTS?

WHAT IS THE WRITTEN (TRANSPOSED) RANGE FOR EACH OF THESE INSTRUMENTS?

WRITE THE FOLLOWING IN THE CORRECT TRANSPOSED KEY FOR EACH INSTRUMENT:

29.
CONCERT KEY:

FOR E♭ ALTO SAX:

FOR B♭ TENOR SAX:

FOR E♭ BARITONE SAX:

WRITE THE FOLLOWING PHRASE FOR THE FOUR BRASS IN THEIR RESPECTIVE KEYS:

30.

FOR TRUMPET I

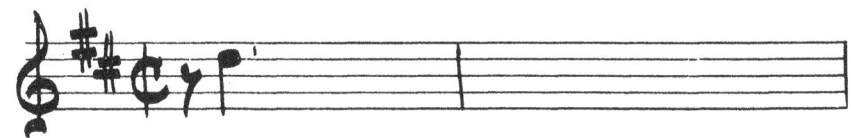

FOR TRUMPET II

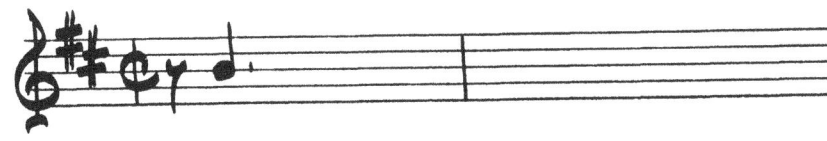

FOR TRUMPET III

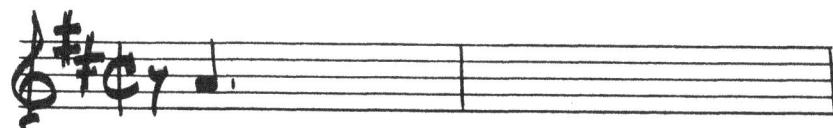

FOR TROMBONE

WRITE THE FOLLOWING PHRASE FOR THREE VIOLINS, VIOLA, AND CELLO:

31.

DANCE BAND HARMONY AND VOICING

BOOK I

DANCE BAND HARMONY AND VOICING

TO BUILD CHORDS YOU MUST KNOW THE SCALES (MAJOR AND MINOR) AND YOU MUST KNOW THE INTERVALS BY NAME.

C MAJOR SCALE:

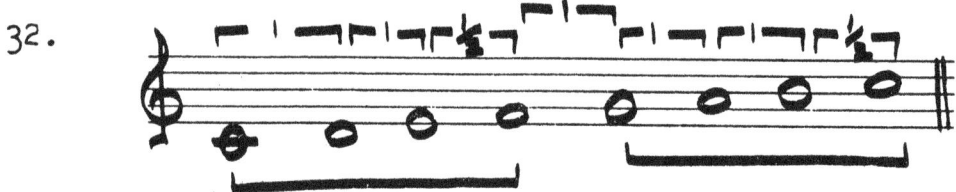

NOTICE THE MAJOR SCALE HAS A HALF STEP BETWEEN THE THIRD AND FOURTH STEPS AND THE SEVENTH AND EIGHTH STEPS. THE REST OF THE INTERVALS ARE ALL WHOLE STEPS.

WRITE MAJOR SCALES ON EVERY NOTE:
C, F, B♭, E♭, A♭, D♭, G♭, F#, B, E, A, D, G, C.

PLAY THEM AND MEMORIZE THEM.

THE A MINOR SCALE (RELATIVE TO C MAJOR)

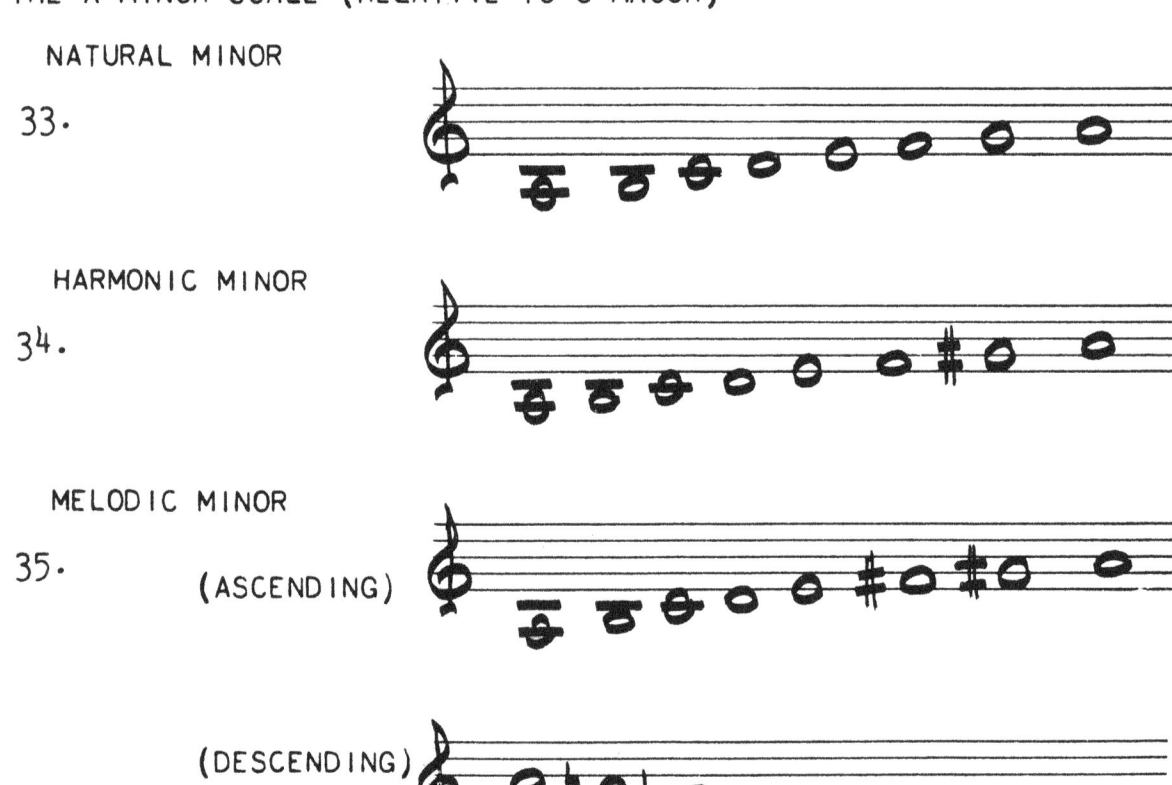

NOTICE THE INTERVALS BETWEEN THE STEPS OF THE DIFFERENT MINOR SCALES.

WRITE MINOR SCALES (HARMONIC MINOR AND MELODIC MINOR) ON THE FOLLOWING NOTES:
A, D, G, C, F, B♭, E♭, D#, G#, C#, F#, B, E, A.

PLAY THEM AND MEMORIZE THEM.

OCCASIONALLY THE HARMONIC MINOR SCALE IS MODIFIED BY RAISING THE 4TH STEP ALSO. THE 2ND STEP MAY BE LOWERED, TOO.

INTERVALS FROM THE NOTE C

36.

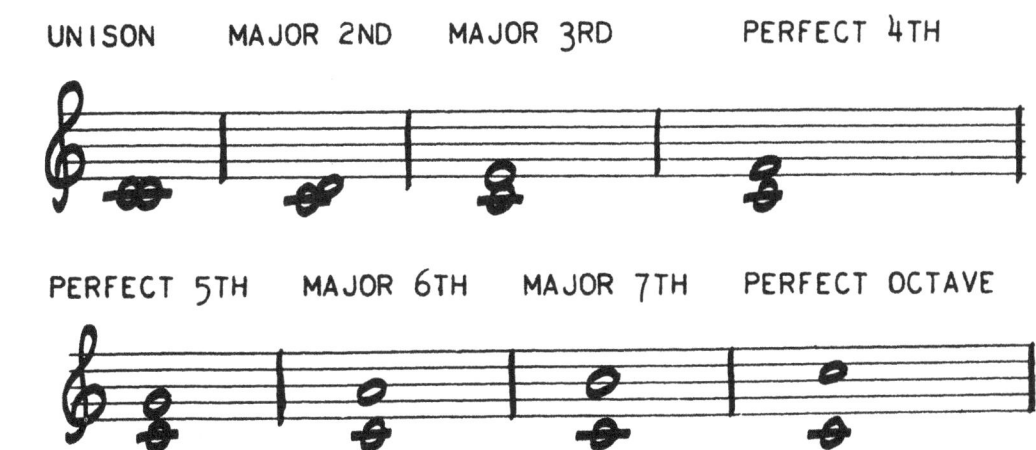

NOTICE TO FIND ANY INTERVAL WE THINK OF THE LOWER NOTE AS THE TONIC (OR ROOT NOTE OF A MAJOR SCALE)
NOTICE THAT 4THS, 5THS, AND OCTAVES ARE CALLED PERFECT INTERVALS.

37.

ANY INTERVAL WHEN MADE LARGER BY A HALF STEP IS CALLED AUGMENTED

38.

ANY <u>MAJOR</u> INTERVAL WHEN MADE SMALLER BY A HALF STEP IS CALLED MINOR

39.
      MIN. 3RD   MIN. 6TH   MIN. 2ND   MIN. 7TH

ANY <u>PERFECT</u> INTERVAL WHEN MADE SMALLER BY A HALF STEP IS CALLED DIMINISHED

40.
      DIM. 5TH   DIM. 4TH   DIM. 5TH   DIM. OCTAVE

ANY MAJOR INTERVAL WHEN MADE SMALLER BY TWO HALF STEPS IS CALLED DIMINISHED

41.
      DIM. 6TH   DIM. 7TH   DIM. 2ND   DIM. 3RD

WRITE THE FOLLOWING INTERVALS ABOVE THE FOLLOWING NOTES (ALWAYS THINKING OF THE LOWER NOTE AS THE TONIC OR 1ST NOTE OF A SCALE)

42.
     PERF. 5TH   MIN. 2ND   AUG. 6TH   DIM. 5TH

     DIM. 7TH   MAJ. 7TH   MIN. 6TH   MIN. 2ND

HARMONY

THREE PART (THREE VOICE) HARMONY:

A MAJOR CHORD HAS:
 A MAJ. 3RD
 A PERF. 5TH
 (FROM THE ROOT)   43.

A MINOR CHORD HAS:
 A MIN. 3RD
 A PERF. 5TH   44.

A DIMINISHED CHORD HAS:
 A DIM. 5TH
 A MIN. 3RD   45.

A DIM. 7TH CHORD HAS:
 A MIN. 3RD
 A DIM. 5TH
 A DIM. 7TH   46.

AN AUG. CHORD HAS:
 A MAJ. 3RD
 AN AUG. 5TH   47.

A DOMINANT 7TH CHORD HAS:
 A MAJ. 3RD
 A PERF. 5TH
 MIN. 7TH   48.
(ALL DOM. 7TH TYPE CHORDS
CONTAIN THE TRITONE-
DIM. 5TH OR AUG. 4TH-)

A DOM. 9TH CHORD IS THE
SAME AS A DOM. 7TH BUT   49.
WITH A MAJ. 9TH ADDED

A DOM. 11+ (RAISED 11TH)
IS THE SAME AS DOM. 9TH   50.
BUT ADD AN AUG. 11TH
(THE AUG. 11TH NOTE OFTEN
SOUNDS LIKE A FLAT FIFTH)

A DOM. 13TH CHORD
(THE 13TH MOST OFTEN
SOUNDS LIKE A SUB-
STITUTE FOR THE 5TH)
(SEE NON-CHORDAL NOTES)

51.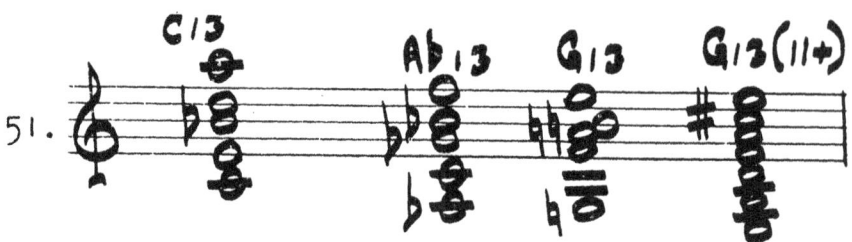

A LOWERED 9TH CHORD
(9-) IS A DOM. 7TH
WITH A MIN. 9TH ADDED

52.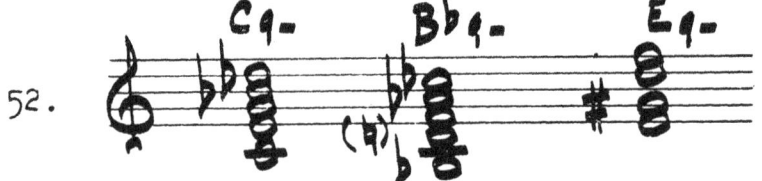

A DOM. 9+ CHORD
(RAISED 9TH) IS A
DOM. 7TH CHORD WITH
AN AUG. 9TH ADDED

53.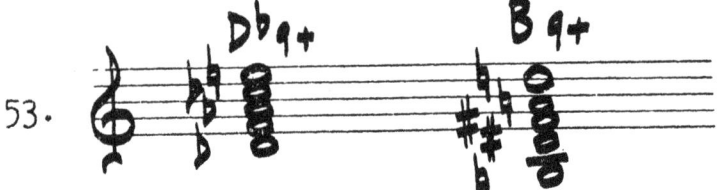

EVEN WHEN THE AUG. 9TH IS
WRITTEN AS A MINOR 10TH
IT IS CUSTOMARY IN
AMERICAN DANCE MUSIC TO
CALL IT A RAISED 9TH CHORD

54.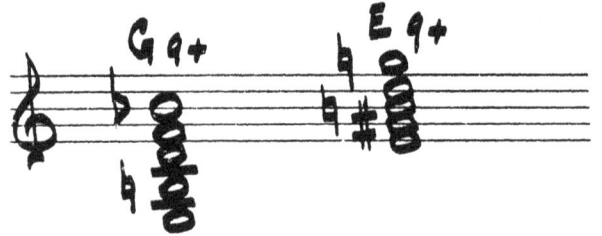

A MIN. 7TH CHORD IS
A MINOR CHORD WITH A
MIN. 7TH ADDED

55.

WHEN USING NON-CHORDAL
NOTES, IT IS NECESSARY TO
NOTATE THE ADDED NOTES
WITH THE CHORD SYMBOL

56.

BUILD THE FOLLOWING CHORDS:

NON-CHORDAL NOTES

(A) SUBSTITUTE NOTES;
  THE NOTE A SCALE STEP ABOVE, OR A HALF STEP BELOW
  (SOMETIMES A SCALE STEP BELOW OR A HALF STEP ABOVE CAN BE
  USED AS A SUBSTITUTE FOR A CHORDAL NOTE.

57.

58.

DO NOT USE THE SUBSTITUTE AND THE REGULAR NOTE OF THE CHORD AT
THE SAME TIME UNLESS THE REGULAR NOTE OF THE CHORD IS OVER AN
OCTAVE BELOW.

59. (NOT TOO GOOD)      (BETTER)

(B) PASSING NOTES;
  NOTES USED IN BETWEEN CHORDAL NOTES

60.

61.

WRITE A SHORT MELODY USING THE DIFFERENT TYPE OF NON-CHORDAL NOTES.

MORE THAN ONE NOTE OF A CHORD CAN BE SUSPENDED. SOMETIMES A WHOLE
CHORD CAN BE SUSPENDED. LIKEWISE WE CAN USE TWO OR MORE PASSING
NOTES AT THE SAME TIME, OR A WHOLE PASSING CHORD MAY BE USED. (SEE 62)

62.

TWO PART HARMONY:
   3RDS AND 6THS SOUND BEST
   2NDS AND 7THS ARE PERMISSABLE
   THE TRITONE MAY BE USED SPARINGLY
   5THS AND 8VES SOUND WEAK
   4THS USUALLY SOUND BAD

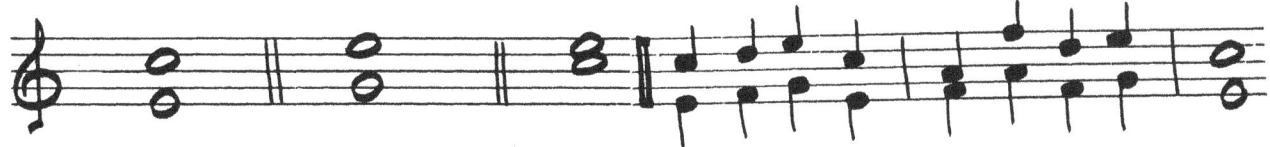

HARMONIZE A POP TUNE WITH TWO PART HARMONY:

THREE PART HARMONY:
   IN A TRIAD (3 NOTE CHORD)
   (MAJ., MIN., DIM., ETC.)
   WE HAVE JUST THREE NOTES TO USE

63.

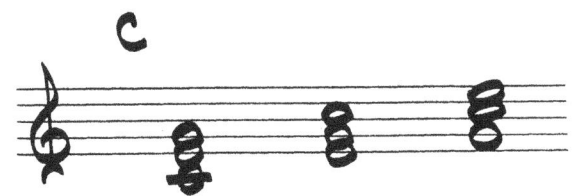

(ALWAYS TREAT NON-CHORDAL NOTES JUST AS IF THEY WERE THE NOTES FOR WHICH THEY ARE SUBSTITUTED)

64.

IN A DOM. 7TH OR DOM. 9TH CHORD, WE HAVE MORE THAN THREE NOTES, SO THE MOST IMPORTANT NOTES IN THE CHORD MUST BE CHOSEN.

65.

EVERY DOM. 7TH CHORD MUST HAVE A THIRD AND A SEVENTH.

FOR A THIRD PART USE EITHER ROOT, 9TH, OR 5TH.

66.

HARMONIZE THE FOLLOWING MELODY WITH THREE PART HARMONY:

67.

FOUR PART TIGHT (BLOCK) HARMONY:
TO MAJ. OR MIN. TRIADS THE MAJ. 6TH,
OR MAJ. 7TH, AND SOMETIMES THE MAJ. 9TH
CAN BE ADDED TO GIVE US THE FOURTH PART.

68.

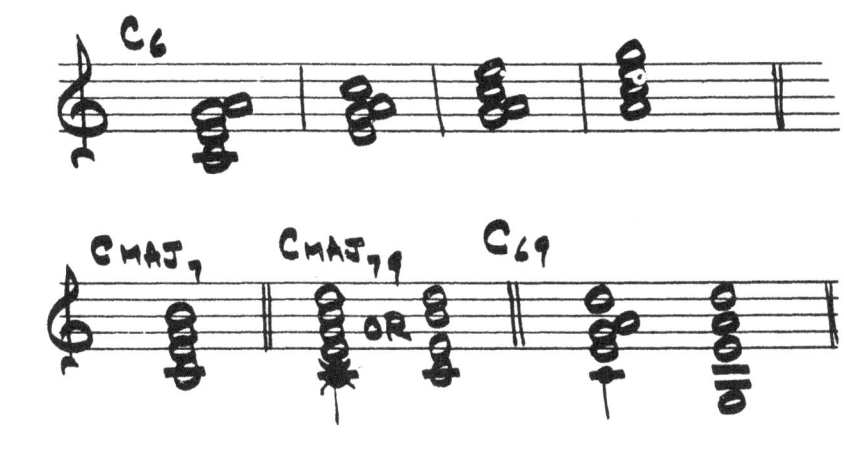

69.

TO DOM. 7TH CHORDS WE MAY ADD THE 9TH INSTEAD OF THE ROOT IN OUR
BLOCK HARMONY.
(DO NOT USE THE 9TH IN THE VERY LOW REGISTER WHERE IT WILL BE A
MAJ. 2ND AWAY FROM THE ROOT OF THE CHORD.)

70.

HARMONIZE ON PAPER THE FOLLOWING PHRASES WITH FOUR PART BLOCK HARMONY. THEN PLAY THEM ON THE PIANO.

71.

72.

WHAT ARE THE MOST IMPORTANT NOTES IN THE DOM. 7TH CHORD?

WHAT NOTES MAY WE ADD TO MAJ. OR MIN. TRIADS TO GIVE US A FOURTH PART IN OUR BLOCK HARMONY?

TAKE ANY PIANO COPY OR LEAD SHEET AND MARK THE CHORD SYMBOLS ABOVE THE MELODY. TO FIND THE ROOT OF A CHORD KEEP INVERTING (OR RE-ARRANGING) THE NOTES OF THE CHORD UNTIL IT IS IN A SERIES OF THIRDS. THE BOTTOM NOTE WILL THEN BE THE ROOT. (ALWAYS TREAT NON-CHORDAL NOTES JUST AS IF THEY WERE THE NOTES THEY ARE SUBSTITUTED FOR) (SEE EX. 263-266, FINDING ROOTS)

TAKE ANY POP TUNE AND WRITE 8 BARS OF IT IN FOUR PART BLOCK STYLE.

IN MAJOR KEYS, WE USUALLY ADD THE MINOR 7TH INTERVAL TO MINOR CHORDS WHEN WE WANT TIGHT HARMONY.

73.

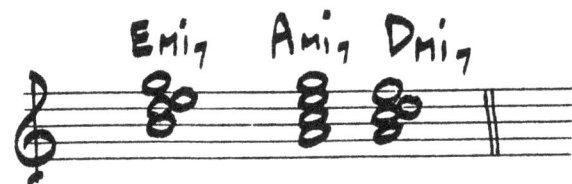

IN MINOR KEYS WE ADD THE MAJOR 6TH OR MAJOR 7TH OR 9TH (AND NOT THE MINOR 7TH TO OUR MINOR CHORDS)

74.

IN MINOR KEYS THE 9TH IN THE V7 CHORD IS A MINOR 9TH.

75.

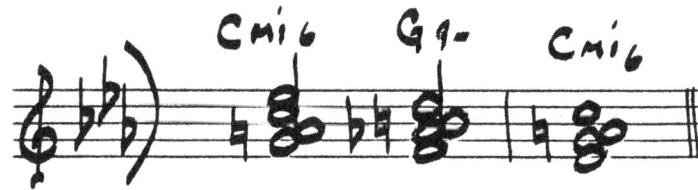

HARMONIZE 8 BARS OF SOME POP TUNE THAT IS IN A MINOR KEY WITH FOUR PART BLOCK HARMONY.

FOUR PART SPREAD (OPEN) HARMONY:
  THE BEST WAY TO OPEN FOUR PART HARMONY IS TO TAKE THE 2ND NOTE FROM THE TOP AND PUT IT ONE OCTAVE LOWER.

76.

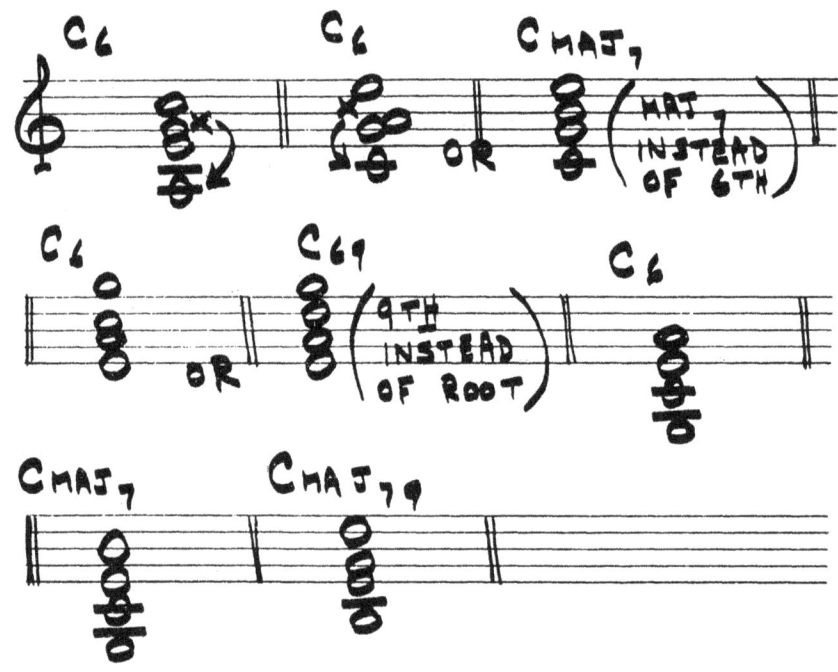

77.

78.

NOTE: WE CAN USE ANY OF THE ♩ NOTES IN (EX. 78-A) WITH ANY OF THE NOTES IN (EX. 78-B) OR VICE VERSA (SEE EX. 78-C FOR SOME OF THE COMBINATIONS)

OPEN A D MI.7 CHORD IN EVERY POSITION (D MELODY, F MELODY, A MELODY, AND C MELODY)

HARMONIZE THE FOLLOWING MELODIES IN FOUR PART OPEN HARMONY:

79. (A)

79. (B)

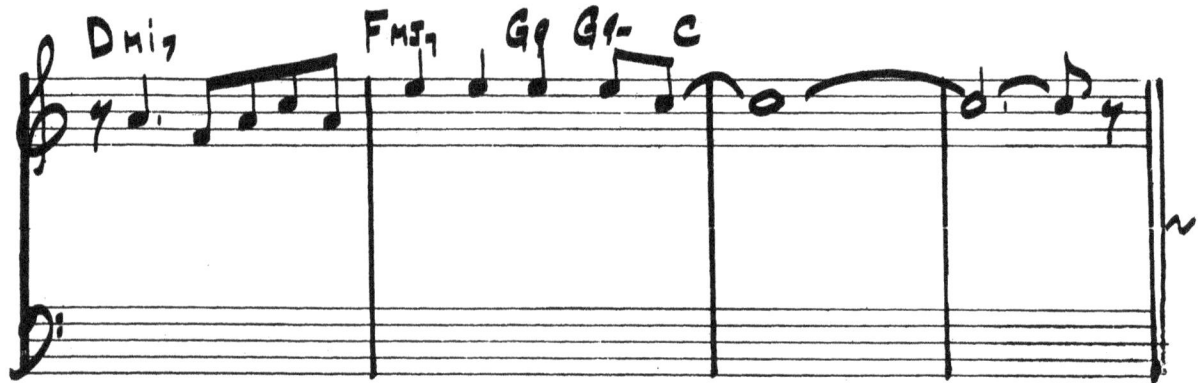

80.

TAKE THE MELODY LINE AND CHORD SYMBOLS OF TWO OR THREE POP TUNES
AND WRITE THEM IN FOUR PART OPEN STYLE.

HARMONIZATION OF NON-CHORDAL NOTES:

IF YOUR GIVEN MELODY IS 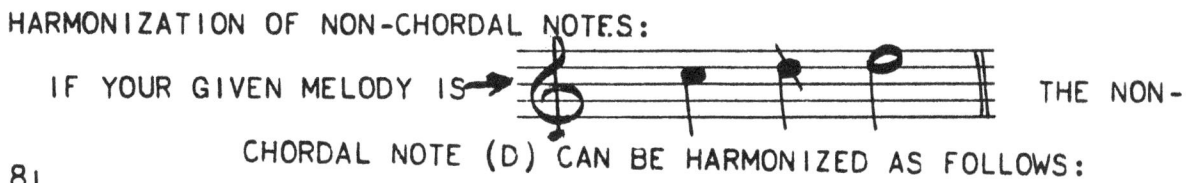 THE NON-CHORDAL NOTE (D) CAN BE HARMONIZED AS FOLLOWS:

81.

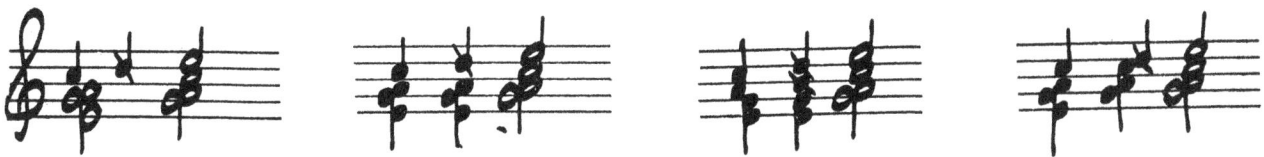

OR WITH ALL FOUR PARTS ON PASSING NOTES WHICH RESULTS IN A PASSING CHORD.

82.

WRITE THE FOLLOWING IN THREE AND FOUR PART BLOCK STYLE USING SOME PASSING CHORDS:

83.

WHEN A NON-CHORDAL NOTE COMES UP TO A CHORDAL NOTE FROM A HALF STEP BELOW, ALL FOUR PARTS MAY ALSO COME FROM A HALF STEP BELOW.

84.

HARMONIZE THE FOLLOWING USING THIS PRINCIPLE:

85.

86.

FIVE OR MORE PARTS:
  CAN BE WRITTEN BLOCK WITH DOUBLED LEAD

87.

OR   SECOND VOICE DOWN AN OCTAVE AND DOUBLED LEAD

88.

OR   OPEN WITH 5TH VOICE ON LOW ROOTS (INSTEAD OF DOUBLED LEAD)

89.

FROM MELODY AND CHORD SYMBOLS OF ANY POP TUNE WRITE:
  5 PART BLOCK - DOUBLED LEAD
  5 PART OPEN - DOUBLED LEAD
  5 PART OPEN - 5TH PART ON LOW ROOTS

FIVE PARTS USING CLUSTERS
  TO MAJOR OR MINOR CHORDS USUALLY THE 6TH AND 9TH ARE ADDED (EX.90)
  SOMETIMES THE 6TH AND MAJOR 7TH (EX.96)

  TO A DOMINANT TYPE CHORD THE 9TH AND ROOT ARE ADDED TO THE
  CLUSTER (EX.90)

90.

FIVE PART CLUSTERS

91.

92.

A 6TH VOICE MAY DOUBLE THE LEAD IN THE NEXT OCTAVE DOWN.

EX. 92 IS THE SAME AS EX. 91 EXCEPT THAT WE STARTED WITH THE 1ST CHORD SPREAD. (FROM THE G DOWN, WE SKIP E AND WRITE D, SKIP C AND WRITE A, SKIP G AND WRITE E, SKIP D AND WRITE C) THIS IS JUST ONE WAY OF SPREADING A CLUSTER, THOUGH IT IS THE MOST USED WAY.

ANOTHER COMMON WAY OF SPREADING A CLUSTER IS TO PUT THE 2ND VOICE FROM THE TOP DOWN AN OCTAVE (EX.93)

93.

WE CAN USE MORE DISSONANCE IF IT IS USED WITH SOME DYNAMIC EFFECT SUCH AS; EXTREME LOUD (FFF), OR EXTREME SOFT (PPP), OR NO VIBRATO, OR FP◄, OR VERY SHORT STACCATO CHORDS.

WRITE 8 BARS OF A POP TUNE USING SPREAD CLUSTERS.

BIG SPREAD CHORDS

MAJOR CHORDS:
   THE NOTES THAT WILL HARMONIZE NORMALLY ARE:
   ROOT, NINTH, THIRD, FIFTH, SIXTH, MAJOR SEVENTH
   AND ON RARE OCCASIONS THE RAISED FOURTH STEP.

94.

VOICINGS:
   WHEN IT IS NECESSARY TO DOUBLE; ROOTS AND FIFTHS ARE THE BEST
   CHOICES THOUGH ANY MELODY NOTE CAN BE DOUBLED IN THE NEXT OCTAVE.

   ROOT AND FIFTH ON THE BOTTOM WILL ALWAYS GIVE YOU A BIG SOUND.
   ROOT, FIFTH, AND TENTH ON BOTTOM WILL ALSO MAKE A SMALL ORCHESTRA
   SOUND LARGE.
   A FOURTH OR FIFTH BETWEEN THE TWO TOP VOICES GIVES A CHORD A
   RING ALSO.

95.

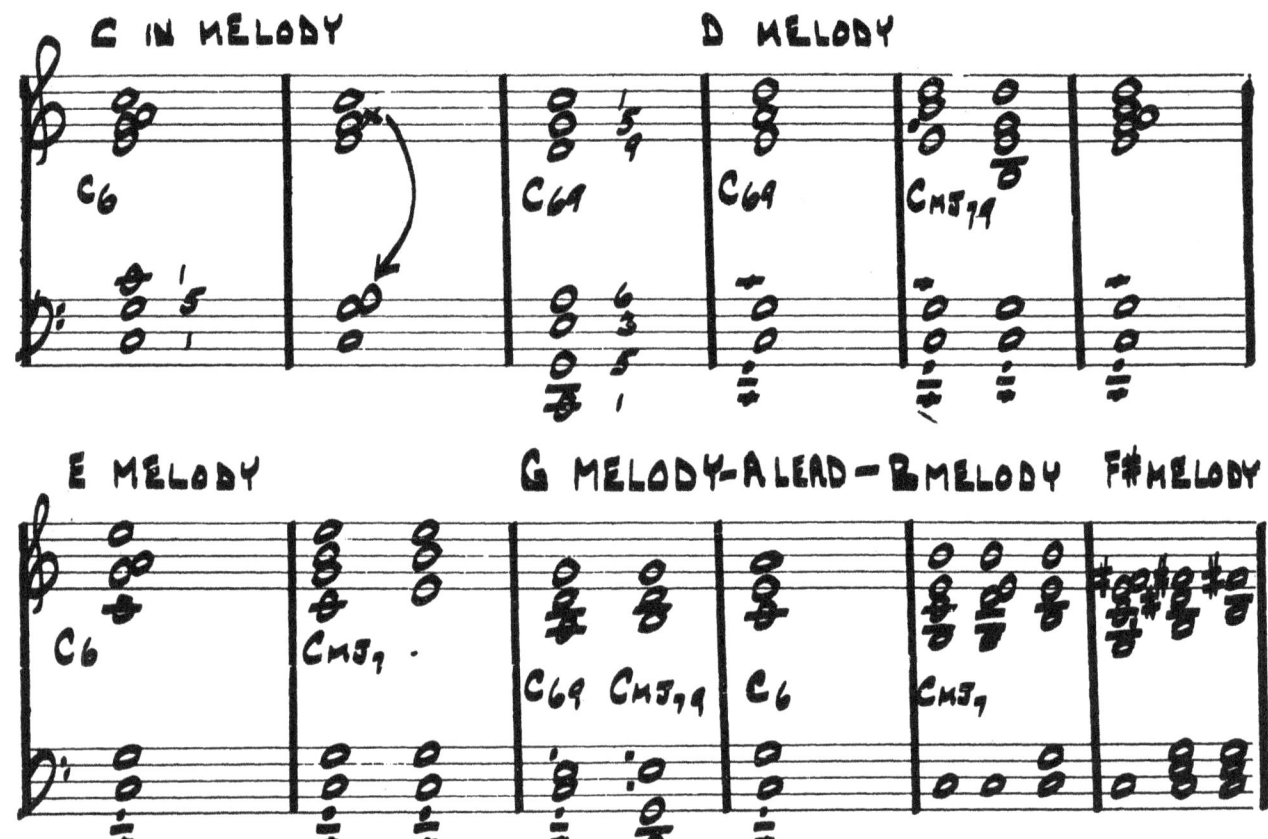

96. HIGH TENSION CLUSTERS:

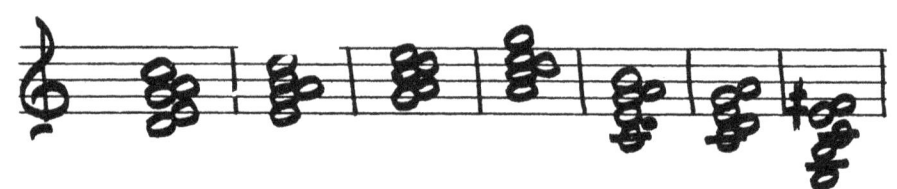

PLAY THESE VOICINGS ON ANY GIVEN ROOT. (EX 95-96)
ALSO PLAY THEM ALL IN C MINOR AND EVERY OTHER MINOR KEY

WRITE THE CLUSTERS (EX 96) IN BIG SPREAD VOICINGS AS WE DID IN EXAMPLE 92 OR 93.

DOMINANT 7TH CHORDS:

IT HAS BECOME A COMMON THING TO SUBSTITUTE FOR ANY DOM. 7TH CHORD THE CHORD BUILT ON IT'S LOWERED FIFTH (FLAT FIFTH) (5-) (D♭ 7TH INSTEAD OF G7)

97.

IF YOU WILL PLAY THE ABOVE CHORDS ON THE PIANO YOU WILL FIND THEM ENHARMONICALLY THE SAME.

THE NOTES MOST FREQUENTLY ALTERED IN THE DOM. 7TH FAMILY ARE THE 5TH AND THE NINTH.

98.

99.

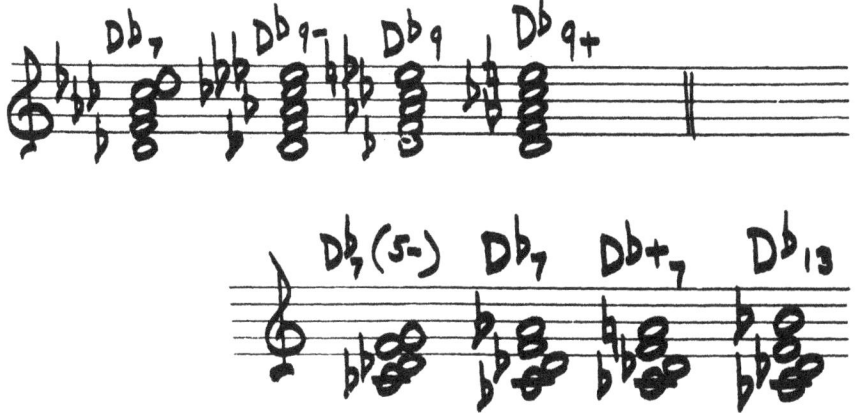

YOU MAY USE COMBINATIONS OF THESE ALTERED 5THS AND 9THS. (EX. 100) (SOME SOUND A LITTLE FALSE BECAUSE OF A SIMULTANEOUS MAJOR MINOR FEELING) IN G 13 (9+), THE NOTE E♮ GIVES A C MAJOR IMPRESSION AND THE NOTE B♭ FEELS LIKE C MINOR.

100.

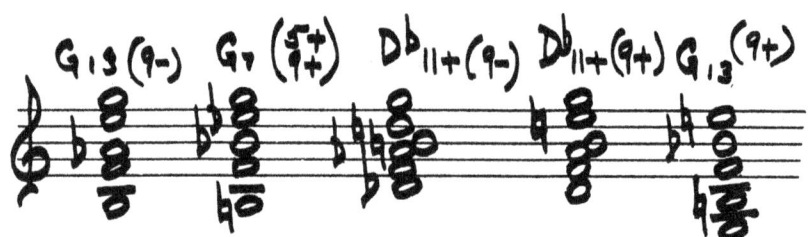

EVERY NOTE IN THE CHROMATIC SCALE WILL HARMONIZE WITH DOM. 7TH CHORD

101.

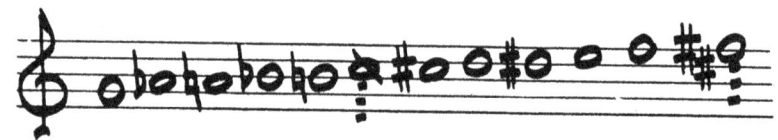

WHAT NOTE OF THE CHORD, IS EACH OF THE ABOVE NOTES (EX. 101) (IN A G7TH?) (IN A D♭ 7TH?)

FOLLOWING ARE SOME OF THE BEST VOICINGS OF A DOM. 7TH AND ITS SUBSTITUTE. WE WILL USE G 7TH AND D♭ 7TH WHICH WILL RESOLVE TO C MAJOR OR C MINOR.

102.

NOTICE ABOVE WE CAN USE ANY OF THE ALTERED 5THS OR 9THS
IN EACH CHORD (OR COMBINATIONS OF THEM) (EX. 98, 99 & 100)

103.

A♭ MELODY

104.

A MELODY

105.

B♭ MELODY

106.

B MELODY

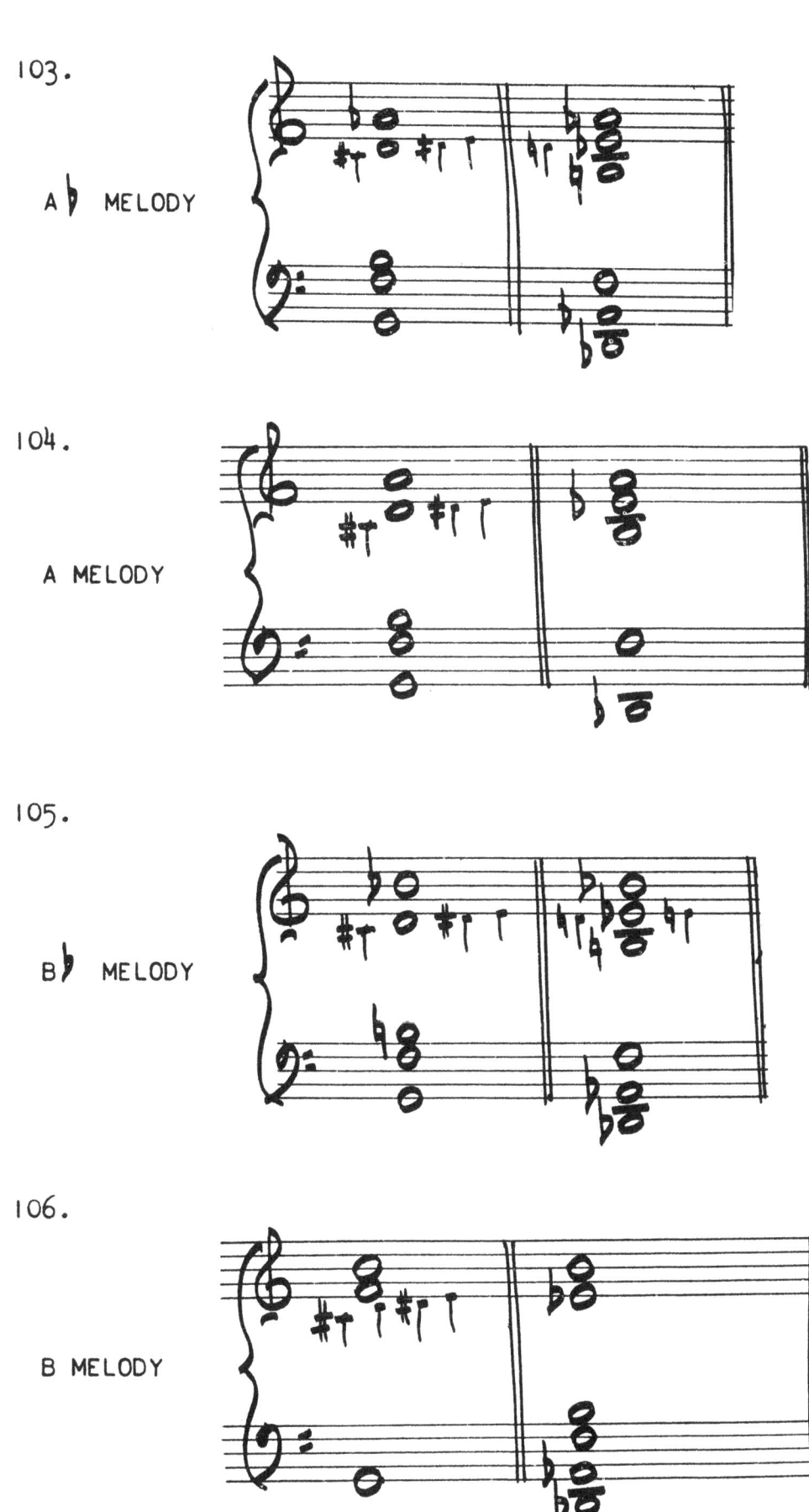

IN EX.106, SECOND BAR, (THE 7TH CAN BE DOUBLED BECAUSE IT IS A MELODY NOTE)

107.

C MELODY

IN EX.107, FIRST BAR, THE NOTE C SOUNDS LIKE A SUSPENSION OF B

108.

C# OR Db MELODY

109.

D MELODY

110.

D# MELODY

WRITE ALL CHORD SYMBOLS FOR EX. 102 THROUGH EX. 113 AND BE ABLE TO PLAY THEM IN ANY KEY AND RESOLVE THEM TO THEIR TONIC CHORDS.

WARNING:

BIG SPREAD CHORDS HAVE MUCH MORE WEIGHT THAN BLOCK CHORDS. ANY MELODY THAT IS SKIPPING AND MOVING VERY FAST IS APT TO SOUND CUMBERSOME IF HARMONIZED WITH BIG SPREAD CHORDS. (IT IS LIKE TRYING TO RUN WITH 150 LBS. ON YOUR BACK)

ALSO BE CAREFUL IN CHANGING FROM THE LIGHT FEELING OF BLOCK STYLE TO THE HEAVIER FEELING OF SPREAD STYLE CHORDS.

THE BEST PLACE TO CHANGE FROM BLOCK STYLE TO SPREAD STYLE IS:

1) AT THE BEGINNING OF A NEW PHRASE OR SECTION
    IE: 1ST 16 BARS SPREAD
         THEN 8 BARS BRIDGE IN BLOCK STYLE ETC.
2) IF YOU ARE BUILDING UP TO HIT A CLIMAX (TOP NOTE IN A PHRASE)
    IT IS A GOOD EFFECT TO SPREAD TO A BIG CHORD ON THE TOP
    CLIMAX NOTE.
3) IF YOU EVER CHANGE FROM BLOCK TO SPREAD OR VICE VERSA IN THE
    MIDDLE OF A PHRASE BE SURE TO DO IT WITH SOME DYNAMIC
    EFFECT. IE: SUDDEN SOFT, SUDDEN LOUD, CHANGE OF COLOR.
4) SUDDEN CHANGE OF REGISTER, AN SFZ, OR AN FP, ETC.

CONSONANCE AND DISSONANCE:

THE MORE COMPLEX THE RATIO OF VIBRATIONS BETWEEN THE NOTES OF AN
INTERVAL THE MORE DISSONANCE (TENSION) IT CREATES.
    (NOTICE THE RATIO OF VIBRATION BETWEEN THE NOTES OF THE
    OCTAVE INTERVAL IS 1 TO 2. THE RATIO OF THE MAJ. 3RD
    INTERVAL IS 4 TO 5. CONSEQUENTLY THE MAJ. 3RD IS RELATIVELY
    MORE DISSONANT THAN THE OCTAVE.)

114.
    CONSONANCE

MILD DISSONANCE   SHARP DISSONANCE   TRITONE (DOM 7TH FEELING)

   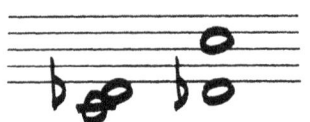   

MEMORIZE EX. 114.

THE TRITONE IS IN A CLASS BY ITSELF. IT GIVES OUR DOM 7TH TYPE CHORD
IT'S DISTINCTIVE FLAVOR.

MUD;
    THE MORE DISSONANT INTERVALS BECOME MUDDY OR OBSCURE IN THE EXTREME
    LOW OR HIGH REGISTERS.

TEST THE FOLLOWING INTERVALS TO SEE HOW LOW YOU CAN WRITE THEM BEFORE THEY BECOME MUDDY. TEST THEM IN THE EXTREME UPPER REGISTER ALSO.
   PERF.5TH, PERF 4TH, MAJ.2ND, MIN.7TH, MAJ.3RD, ETC

IN DIATONIC (TONAL) MUSIC:
   THE MORE DISSONANT A CHORD IS THE SMOOTHER IT MUST RESOLVE!!!

   EACH NOTE RESOLVES BY A HALF STEP, A WHOLE STEP, OR STAYS COMMON, OR MOVES BY A PERFECT INTERVAL (PERF 5TH, PERF.4TH, PERF 8VE)

   ALTERED NOTES (NOTES OUT OF THE SCALE OF OUR KEY) MUST RESOLVE SMOOTHLY!!

SOME PRETTY NOTES AGAINST THE DIFFERENT TYPE CHORDS. THESE NOTES ADD TENSION AND GIVE YOUR MUSIC MOTION.

115.
   AGAINST THE DOM 7TH

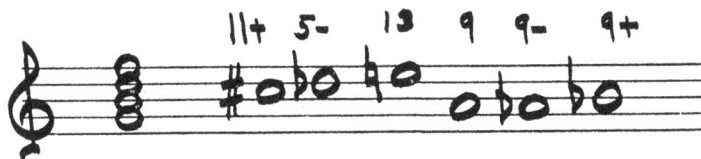

116.
   AGAINST THE MAJ. CHORD

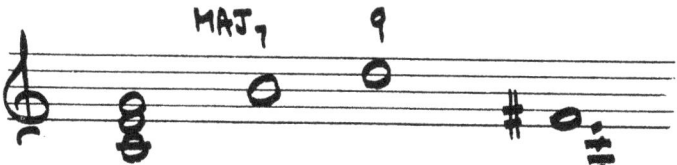

117.
   AGAINST THE MIN. CHORD

118.
   AGAINST THE MIN.7TH CHORD

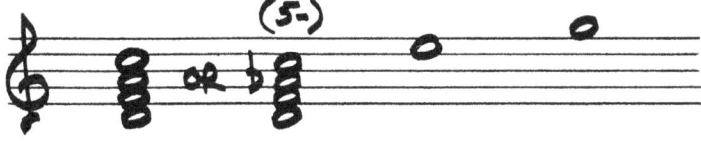

119.
AGAINST AUG. CHORD

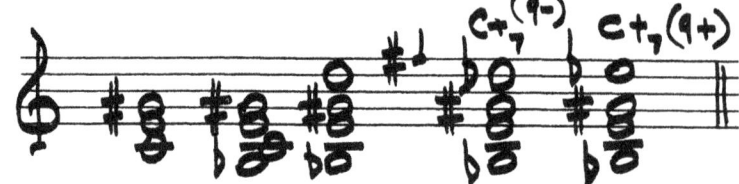

120.
AGAINST DIM. CHORD

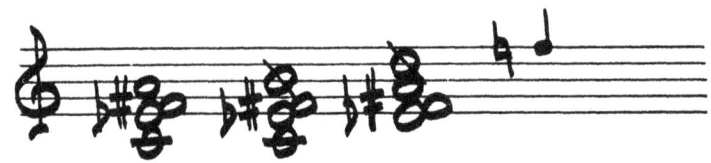

WRITE A MELODIC LINE OVER THE FOLLOWING CHORDS USING SOME OF THE NOTES AGAINST THE CHORDS THAT ARE SUGGESTED ABOVE:

121.

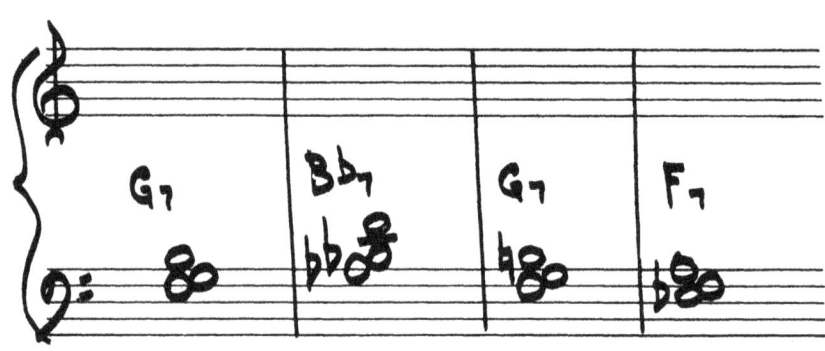

RESOLVE ALL THE DOM 7TH TYPE CHORDS IN EX 102 TO 113 TO A TONIC (MAJ. OR MIN. CHORD) G 7TH TO C --- Db 7TH TO C.
HARMONIZE THE FOLLOWING EXERCISES:

122.

BE ABLE TO TELL WHICH OF ANY TWO CHORDS IS THE MOST DISSONANT AND WHY.

A KNOWLEDGE OF SOLFEGE (DO, RE, MI, FA, SOL, LA, TI, DO, ETC.,)
WILL SPEED UP YOUR WRITING 700 OR 800 PERCENT.
   IE: IF YOU WANT TO WRITE THE FOLLOWING PHRASE (EX.123) FOR ALTO
       SAX, INSTEAD OF TRANSPOSING EACH INDIVIDUAL NOTE UP A MAJ.6TH,
       YOU CAN SING A PHRASE AT A TIME AND THEN WRITE THE PHRASE IN
       THE ALTO SAX KEY.
  YOU MUST KNOW YOUR SOLFEGE (MOVEABLE DO) IN EACH KEY.

123.

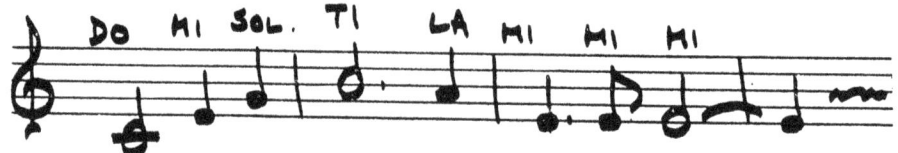

THE ALTO SAX IS IN THE KEY OF A MAJ. SO; DO, MI, SOL, TI, LA, MI, MI,
MI WOULD BE:

124.

SOLFEGE WILL ALSO ENABLE YOU TO WRITE AWAY FROM THE PIANO WHICH SPEEDS
UP YOUR WRITING. LOTS OF GOOD ARRANGERS HAVE TO WRITE WITH PIANO
BUT THE PRESENT DAY DEMAND FOR SPEED IN COMMERCIAL WRITING PUTS THEM
AT A DISADVANTAGE.

LEARN ALL YOUR CHORDS BY SYLLABLES.
ALSO WITH SOLFEGE YOU CAN LEARN TO WRITE AN ARRANGEMENT FOR DANCE
BAND WITHOUT SCORE. (JUST WRITING THE PARTS) THIS IS NOT ADVISABLE
UNTIL YOU ARE A THOROUGHLY EXPERIENCED ARRANGER.

WHEN WRITING AN ARRANGEMENT WITHOUT A SCORE, WRITE THE LEAD TRUMPET
AND THE LEAD SAX PARTS ALL THE WAY THROUGH AND REMEMBER WHERE YOU
WANT BLOCK HARMONY AND WHERE YOU WANT OPEN VOICING.

125.

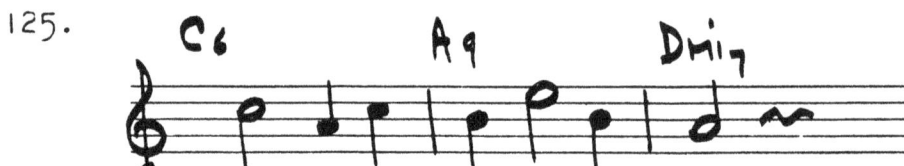

C CHORD (DO,MI,SOL,LA)
A CHORD (DI,MI,SOL,TI -LA BASS-)
D MIN.7TH (RE,FA,LA,DO)

IN ENSEMBLE:
  TRPT I WILL PLAY
  DO,LA,DO,TI,MI,TI,LA,
  IN THE KEY OF D MAJ.

TRPT II WILL PLAY NEXT PART
LA,SOL,LA,SOL,DI,SOL,FA

TRPT III WILL PLAY NEXT PART
UNDER 2ND TRPT.
SOL,MI,SOL,MI,TI,TI,MI,RE

TROMBONE WILL PLAY
MI,DO,MI,DI,SOL,DI,DO

THE SAXES CAN BE DONE THE SAME WAY. DOUBLING LEAD ALTO WITH LEAD TRPT
ISN'T USUALLY DONE EXCEPT IN CERTAIN STYLE BANDS THAT SOUND VERY MUCH
OUT OF TUNE.

WAYS OF PRACTICING SOLFEGE:
1) SIGHT SING
2) LISTEN TO MUSIC AND TRY TO HEAR WHAT SYLLABLES THE MELODY NOTES ARE.
3) TRY TO TELL WHAT NOTE OF THE CHORD IS IN THE MELODY (3RD,5TH,11TH, 13TH, ETC.)
4) TAKE ANY TUNE YOU KNOW AND SING THE SYLLABLES TO IT.
5) HAVE SOMEONE PLAY OR SING MELODIES AND WRITE THEM DOWN.
6) PRACTICE TRANSPOSING BY SOLFEGE.
7) PRACTICE INTERVAL RECOGNITION (MAJ.3RD,MIN.6TH,ETC.)
8) LEARN TO RECOGNIZE ALL THE CHORDS BY THEIR SOUND. (MAJ,MIN,AUG, DIM,DIM.7TH,MAJ.7TH,MIN.7TH,MAJ.69,11TH+,13TH,9+, ETC.)
9) WHEN YOU PLAY OR SING (EVEN WHEN IT'S A 3RD OR 4TH VOICE) THINK WHAT SYLLABLES YOUR NOTES ARE AND WHAT NOTE OF THE CHORD YOU ARE PLAYING.
10) COPY RECORDS.
    IF YOU CAN HEAR THE SYLLABLES YOU CAN WRITE THE LEAD LINES (MELODIES) DOWN (1ST TRPT AND 1ST SAX)
    IF YOU CAN FEEL WHAT NOTE OF THE CHORD EACH MELODY IS THEN YOU KNOW WHAT THE CHORDS ARE.
      (OR IF YOU HAVE TROUBLE HEARING CHORDS, LISTEN TO THE BASS LINE)

IF YOU KNOW WHAT CHORDS TO EXPECT NEXT IT HELPS.
(SEE EX.269; LOGICAL ROOT PROGRESSION)
YOU CAN TELL WITH A LITTLE PRACTICE WHERE THE ARRANGER
USED BLOCK HARMONY AND WHERE HE USED OPEN HARMONY.
IF YOU KNOW ALL THIS IT IS A MATTER OF WRITING IT DOWN
ON A SKETCH AND THEN SCORING (OR WRITING THE PARTS
DIRECTLY FROM THE SKETCH)

IF YOU HAVE TROUBLE WRITING DOWN CORRECT RHYTHMS, <u>SUBDIVIDE!</u>
IF YOU HEARD THE PHRASE

126.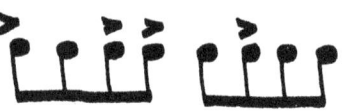

AND DIDN'T KNOW WHAT IT LOOKED LIKE ON PAPER;
WRITE A BAR OF EIGHTH NOTES (126-A) AND TAPPING OFF ALL EIGHT
EVENLY, SING THE PHRASE YOU WANT TO WRITE DOWN, AND FIND WHICH
OF THE EIGHTH NOTES THE ACCENTS OF YOUR PHRASE FALL ON.
   IE: TAPPING THE FOLLOWING EIGHTH NOTES OUT EVENLY,
       YOU WILL FIND THAT THE NOTES IN EX.126 FALL ON THE
       1ST, 3RD, 4TH, AND 6TH EIGHTH NOTES.

126-A

WHICH GIVES US

ALWAYS WRITE RHYTHMS SO THAT OUR EYE CAN DIVIDE THE BAR IN HALF

IE: ♩ ♫♪♪ ♩.   NOT   ♩ ♪♩ ♩.

IE: ♪♩. ♩. ♪   NOT   ♪♩. ♪

RHYTHM IS THE MOST BASIC ELEMENT IN MUSIC.

   IT IS THE MOST EMOTION AROUSING PART OF MUSIC.
   EVEN IN A SLOW BALLAD THE RHYTHM OF THE MELODY AND THE
   COUNTER MELODIES ARE ALL IMPORTANT.

   ALWAYS MAKE RHYTHM YOUR FIRST CONSIDERATION!
   FORM IS JUST RHYTHM ON A LARGER SCALE.

   CONSIDER ALSO THE RHYTHM OF YOUR CHORD CHANGES.
   THE RHYTHM OF THE ENTRANCE OF INSTRUMENTS OR SECTIONS IS ALSO
   IMPORTANT.

MELODY IS SECOND IN IMPORTANCE.

HARMONY AND VOICING COME THIRD.

   EVEN THOUGH WE ARRANGERS LOVE BEAUTIFUL CHORDS AND VOICINGS,
   REMEMBER RHYTHM AND MELODIC LINE COME FIRST.

TIMBRE AND COLOR (ORCHESTRATION) ARE THE FOURTH CONSIDERATION

       THE WAY WE HANDLE THE ABOVE FOUR ELEMENTS GIVES US THE
       MOOD AND FEELING WE ARE TRYING TO CREATE IN THE LISTENERS
       MIND.

FORM
(PLANNING AN ARRANGEMENT)

BOOK II

PLAN OF AN ARRANGEMENT (FORM)

FIRST BECOME FAMILIAR WITH THE MELODY AND HARMONY OF THE COMPOSITION YOU ARE GOING TO ARRANGE. READ THE LYRICS (IF ANY) AND FIND OUT WHAT MOOD THE TUNE IS SUPPOSED TO CONVEY. PLAY THE TUNE. SING IT OUT LOUD!!

DECIDE WHAT INSTRUMENTS IT IS BEST SUITED FOR. SOME TUNES ARE BEST AS SOLO - SOME SOUND BEST AS AN ENSEMBLE, OR WITH A BRASS SECTION, OR AS A SAX SOLI   (LISTEN TO BANDS ON RECORD OR IN PERSON AND NOTICE WHAT TYPE OF THINGS SOUND BEST IN BRASS OR IN SAXES, ETC.)

LEARN TO LISTEN ANALYTICALLY!! YOU WILL NOTICE THAT BRASS ARE ABLE TO PUNCH THINGS MUCH MORE THAN SAXES - AND SAXES CAN PLAY A MOVING LEGATO PASSAGE MUCH MORE GRACEFULLY THAN BRASS CAN.

WRITE FOR THE INSTRUMENTS!! DON'T PLAY OR WRITE SOMETHING THAT MAY BE GOOD ON THE PIANO AND EXPECT IT TO SOUND THE SAME ON AN INSTRUMENT THAT IS BLOWN OR BOWED. WRITE WITH THE INSTRUMENT IN MIND THAT IS GOING TO PLAY IT

SKETCH OUT A FEW BARS OF THE TUNE IN AS MANY WAYS AS YOU CAN THINK OF, THEN DECIDE WHICH IDEAS BELONG IN WHAT PART OF THE ARRANGEMENT.

YOU WILL FIND THAT ARRANGING IS JUST LIKE PUTTING A JIG SAW PUZZLE TOGETHER EXCEPT THAT YOU HAVE TOO MANY PIECES (OR IDEAS) AND SOME WILL HAVE TO BE THROWN OUT IF THEY DON'T FIT INTO THE PICTURE AS A WHOLE

CREATIVE IMAGINATION, INSPIRATION, AND INTUITION WILL DEVELOP AND BECOME MORE FLUENT WITH PRACTICE.

WRITE DOWN THE PLAN OF YOUR ARRANGEMENT, AND START YOUR SKETCH . WRITE THE FIRST CHORUS. (IN SKETCH -TWO LINE, OR FOUR IF YOU NEED IT-

THEN WRITE THE INTRODUCTION. YOU CAN'T INTRODUCE SOMETHING UNTIL YOU KNOW IT. YOU WILL ALWAYS GET LOTS OF IDEAS FOR YOUR INTRO FROM SOME MELODIC LINE, OR COUNTER MELODY, OR RHYTHM, OR HARMONIC PROGRESSION, OR VOICING THAT OCURRS IN YOUR FIRST CHORUS. (SEE INTROS, INTERLUDES, AND MODULATIONS)

WHEN YOUR SKETCH IS COMPLETED THEN SCORE IT (TRANSPOSED) OR SOME ARRANGERS CAN COPY THE PARTS DIRECTLY FROM THE SKETCH.

PROCEDURE:

1) BECOME FAMILIAR WITH TUNE (PLAY IT, SING IT, READ THE LYRICS)
2) SKETCH A FEW BARS IN AS MANY WAYS AS YOU CAN
3) WRITE DOWN THE PLAN OF THE WHOLE ARRANGEMENT.
4) SKETCH IT
5) SCORE IT
6) HAVE IT COPIED
7) HAVE IT PLAYED
8) LISTEN TO IT ANALYTICALLY AND LEARN FROM IT
9) THEN START ANOTHER ONE
10) WRITE AND WRITE AND WRITE!!

ON THE FOLLOWING PAGES ARE EXAMPLES OF THIS PROCEDURE;

PEOPLE CAN ONLY HEAR TWO IDEAS AT ONCE. (UNLESS THEY HAVE MORE THAN ONE HEAD)
   IE: SAXES AGAINST BRASS; BRASS AGAINST SAXES; SOLO AGAINST BG
       (BACKGROUND), ETC.
IF YOU USE MORE THAN TWO IDEAS SIMILTANEOUSLY BE SURE THAT ALL BUT TWO ARE SUBSERVIENT TO THE REST AT ANY ONE TIME.

   SOME POTENTIAL POSSIBILITIES ARE:
        ENSEMBLES
        SECTIONS
        SOLOS   WITH OR WITHOUT BG
        UNISONS

   BG (BACKGROUND) CAN BE:
        ORGAN (GOOP) - OR A UNISON LINE - OR RHYTHM PATTERNS
        OR FILL INS (COMING IN INTERMITTENTLY)

SUPPOSE OUR ORCHESTRA HAS:

                    BRASS   -   3 TRPTS
                                TROMBONE

                    SAXES   -   2 ALTOS
                                2 TENORS

                    RHYTHM -   PIANO
                                BASS
                                DRUMS
                                GUITAR

SOME OF OUR POSSIBILITIES WOULD BE:

1) ENSEMBLE
    A) BRASS SECTION LEAD
       SAX BG

127.

BRASS IS BLOCK HARMONY IN EX. 127 (THE SECOND VOICE FROM THE TOP IS PULLED DOWN AN OCTAVE, THOUGH IT IS NOT NECESSARY)

BG CAN BE ORGAN WHOLE NOTES (GOOP)

128.

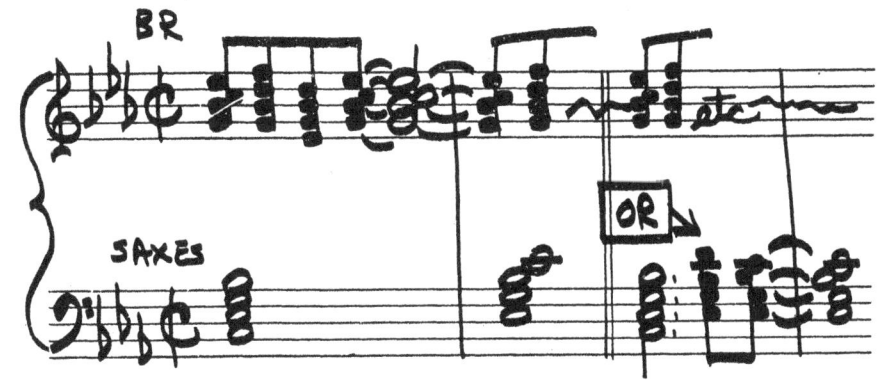

THE STUDENT SHOULD WRITE DEEP ORGAN BACKGROUND (GOOP) TO SEVERAL POP TUNES. (THOSE WHO HAVE STUDIED "LEGITIMATE" HARMONY AND COUNTERPOINT HAVE A DECIDED ADVANTAGE HERE)

BG CAN BE UNISON OR OCTAVES (SINCE BRASS IS COMPLETE HARMONICALLY)

129.

IT IS ALWAYS GOOD TO <u>CONTRAST</u> THE <u>BG</u> <u>AGAINST</u> THE <u>MELODY</u>.

1) <u>RHYTHMICALLY</u>:
   IF MELODY IS HOLDING A NOTE THE BG CAN MOVE IN FASTER RHYTHMS AND WHEN MELODY IS MOVING THE BG SHOULD NOT MOVE TOO MUCH. (SEE EX. 127)

2) <u>CONTRAST IN COLOR</u>:
   IF BRASS HAS MELODY GIVE ANOTHER SECTION THE BG OR VICE VERSA.

3) <u>CONTRAST IN REGISTER</u>:
   NOTE IN EX. 127 TO 129 THE BRASS IS FAIRLY HIGH SO THAT THE SAX BG IS IN THE LOWER REGISTER.

4) <u>CONTRAST THICK AND THIN</u>:
   IN EX. 129 THE BRASS IS THICK (BLOCK OR OPEN) AND SAXES ARE THIN (UNISON)

   LEAD LINE OF BG SHOULD ALWAYS STAY AWAY FROM MELODY OF TUNE.
   IE: TOP SAX STAYS AWAY FROM TOP TRPT NOTES IN EX. 127, 128, & 129 ETC. - THE TOP LINE OF THE BG IS ACTUALLY A COUNTERPOINT AGAINST THE MELODY.

ENSEMBLE
    B) BRASS OCTAVE LEAD
       SAX BG

130.

ENSEMBLE
    C) BRASS AND SAXES ALL WORKING TOGETHER
       OVERLAPPING (USED ON STOCKS OR FOR ARRANGEMENTS
       THAT MAY BE PLAYED BY LARGE OR SMALL ORCH.)

131.

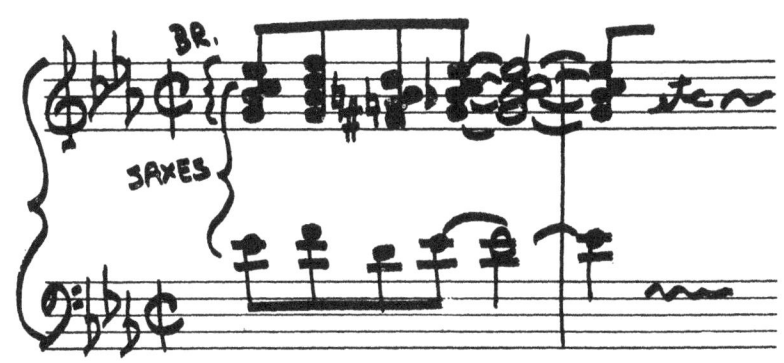

(OVERLAP:)
NOTICE IN ALL THESE EXAMPLES THERE IS NEVER A PLACE WHERE ONE SECTION (OR SOLO) STOPS BEFORE THE OTHER STARTED. THIS MAKES FOR SMOOTH TRANSITIONS AND GIVES ARRANGEMENT MORE FLOW OR CONTINUITY.

(SEE EX. 127 TO 138)

132.

133.

2) SOLO WITH BG

134.

EX.134 COULD ALSO BE WRITTEN AS TROMBONE SOLO WITH SAME BG OR
AS PIANO SOLO OR GUITAR SOLO WITH SAME BG (OR BG COULD BE CLARINETS)

135.

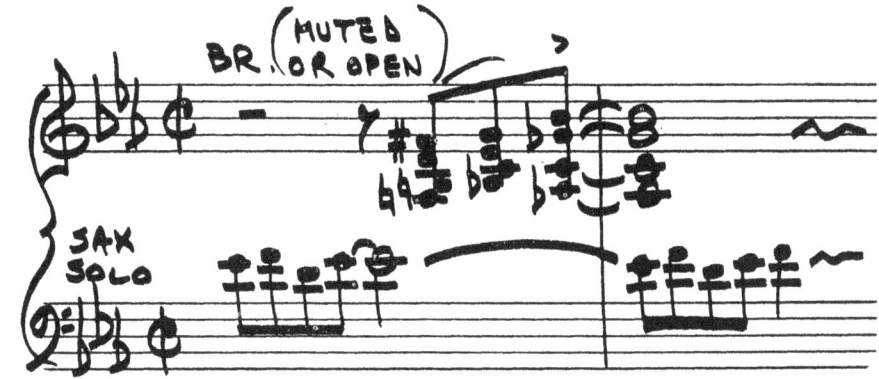

3) SAX SECTION WITH BG (EX. 136 137)

136.

137.

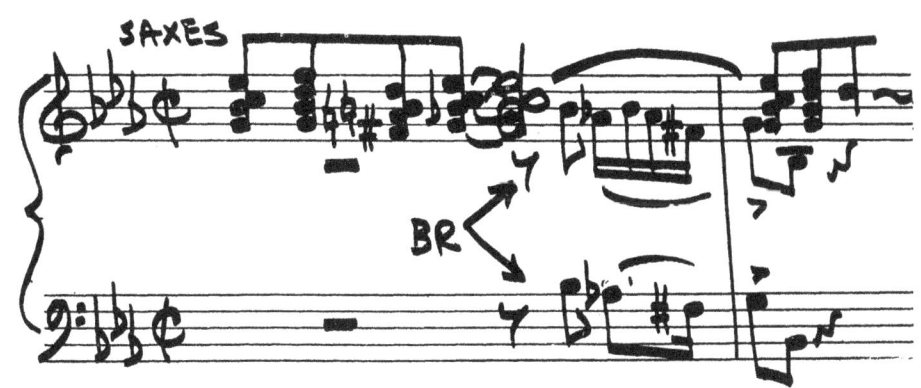

4) SAX UNISON WITH BRASS BG (EX 138)

138.

5) OTHER COLORS
   A) TROMBONE LEAD WITH SAX HARMONY (OR CLAR. HARMONY)

139.

(SOME OR ALL OF THE SAXES CAN BE ABOVE THE TROM LEAD WITHOUT COVERING HIM UP)

   B) TENOR SAX LEAD WITH SAX HARMONY

140.
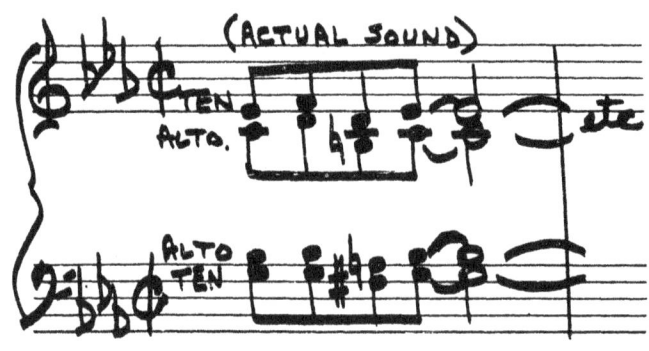

   C) CLAR. LEAD WITH SAXES (OFTEN CALLED MILLER STYLE)
      (BEST RANGE FOR CLAR. LEAD IS BETWEEN CONCERT A IN THE STAFF AND HIGH C OR HIGH D)

141.
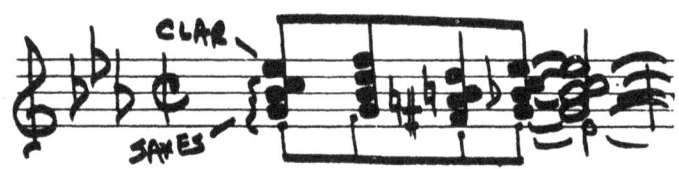

   D) TROM. LEAD WITH TRPTS ON HARMONY ABOVE HIM (OR BELOW, OR BOTH)
      (VERY EFFECTIVE WITH TROM. IN SOLOTONE MUTE AND TRPTS IN CUPS)

142.

E) ANY COMBINATION OF BRASS WITH CLARS (EITHER BRASS ON LEAD, OR CLAR. LEAD)
F) ANY COMBINATION OF ELECTRIC GUITAR WITH CLARS. OR ELECTRIC GUITAR WITH CLARS. AND MUTED BRASS.
G) ANY OF OUR SMALL COMBOS CAN BE USED WITHIN AN ARRANGEMENT FOR LARGER ORCHESTRA.
H) TROM CAN BE USED INDEPENDENTLY OF TRPTS IF DESIRED (EX. 143)

143

I) TROM COULD HAVE LEAD (AS SOLO OR WITH SAX HARMONY, EX. 107) AND ONE TRPT (AD LIB OR WRITTEN) BG (OR THREE TRPT UNISON NO VIBRATO FILLS)

144.

(NOTICE EACH COLOR HAS ITS OWN INDEPENDENT PERSONALITY IN EX. 143, 144)

THERE ARE MANY MORE POSSIBILITIES BUT THESE ARE THE MOST DEPENDABLE. USE THE MIXED OR ODD COMBINATIONS (MIXTURES OF COLORS) SPARINGLY. LET YOUR ENSEMBLES, SOLOS, PURE SECTIONS, AND UNISONS BE THE BASIS OF YOUR ARRANGEMENTS AND USE THE MIXTURES FOR OCCASIONAL CONTRAST.

TAKE ANY POP TUNE AND SKETCH 3 OR 4 BARS IN AS MANY WAYS AS YOU CAN FOR:
4 BRASS, 4 SAXES, AND 4 RHYTHM.

AFTER YOU HAVE DONE THIS YOU WILL SEE THAT YOU HAVE ENOUGH MATERIAL FOR SEVERAL ARRANGEMENTS.

TRY TO BUILD YOUR ARRANGEMENT OUT OF AS FEW IDEAS AS POSSIBLE. ALL BEGINNERS USE TOO MANY IDEAS. IT HURTS TO THROW OUT A GOOD IDEA, BUT IF IT DOESN'T FIT IN THE PICTURE OF THE ARRANGEMENT AS A WHOLE, THROW IT OUT OR SAVE IT FOR ANOTHER TIME. MANY ARRANGERS KEEP A MUSICAL NOTEBOOK FULL OF IDEAS FOR FUTURE USE.

AFTER YOU HAVE SKETCHED 4 BARS OR SO IN AS MANY WAYS AS YOU CAN THEN PLAN THE WHOLE ARRANGEMENT.

YOU MAY LOOK AT YOUR SKETCHES AND DECIDE ONE IDEA IS A GOOD IDEA FOR YOUR FIRST CHORUS. ANOTHER WILL BE JUST RIGHT FOR THE CLIMAX. (USUALLY IN THE LAST CHORUS)

THERE ARE THREE GENERAL PLANS FOR A POP TUNE ARRANGEMENT:

PLAN - 1

1ST CHORUS ---
- 16 BARS - ENSEMBLE
- 8 BARS - SAXES (OR SOLO)
- 8 BARS - ENSEMBLE

2ND CHORUS ---
- 8 BARS - SOLO (PIANO, OR SAX, OR CLAR)
- 8 BARS - SOLO (SAME)
- 8 BARS - SECTION (BRASS OR SAXES)
- 8 BARS - SOLO

LAST CHORUS ---
(HIGHER KEY)
- 16 BARS - ENSEMBLE
- 8 BARS - SOLO
- 8 BARS - ENSEMBLE

YOU CAN SEE THAT PLAN I IS:
  1ST CHORUS MOSTLY ENSEMBLE, FULL AND BIG
  2ND CHORUS THINS OUT TO SOLOS
  3RD CHORUS FULL BIG ENSEMBLE TOPS 1ST CHORUS BY BEING IN A HIGHER KEY.

VERY OFTEN THIS LAST CHORUS IS ONLY 16 BARS AND OUT.
(ON A SINGLE RECORD THEY WANT TO KEEP THE TIME BETWEEN 2:15 AND 2:45) (OR 3 MINUTES AT THE MOST)

PLAN- 2

1ST CHORUS	---	MOSTLY SOLO
2ND CHORUS	---	SECTIONS
3RD CHORUS (HIGHER KEY)	---	ENSEMBLE

VERY OFTEN WE END RIGHT ON THE CLIMAX AND LET THE AUDIENCE TAPER IT OFF WITH THEIR APPLAUSE.

PLAN 2 STARTS THIN AND GRADUALLY BUILDS TO A BIG CLIMAX NEAR THE END. THIS PLAN WORKS NICELY WITH TUNES THAT BUILD RHYTHMICALLY AND MELODIC LY A LA BOLERO. MAMBOS AND RIFF TUNES (OVER THE BLUES PROGRESSION) WILL FIT INTO THIS FORM NICELY.

PLAN- 3

THIS IS WONDERFUL IF YOU HAVE SOME NICE EFFECT TO START YOUR FIRST CHORUS IE: BRASS UNISON (NO VIBRATO A LA FRENCH HORN) WITH DEEP SAX ORGAN BG AND PIANO FILLS A LA SOFT CHIMES.

1ST CHORUS	---	16 BARS - EFFECT 8 BARS - SECTION 8 BARS - EFFECT
2ND CHORUS (HIGHER KEY)	---	16 BARS - ENSEMBLE 8 BARS - SOLO (OR SECTION) 8 BARS - ENSEMBLE
3RD CHORUS (ORIGINAL KEY)	---	8 OR 16 BARS - EFFECT AND OUT

PLAN 3 IS VERY NICE BECAUSE IT RETURNS TO THE BEGINNING IDEA AT THE END, WHICH IS ONE OF THE BASIC PRINCIPALS IN FORM (ALSO IN ALL LIFE). FORM IS JUST RHYTHM ON A LARGER SCALE.

EVERY TUNE WILL ASK FOR A VARIATION OF ONE OF THESE THREE PLANS BUT BASICALLY THEY WILL BE THE ROUGH FRAMEWORK FOR ALL YOUR ARRANGING.

IN EACH OF THESE PLANS THE CLIMAX WILL BE 2/3 OR 3/4 OR 4/5 (APPROX) OF THE WAY THROUGH.

MOST VOCAL SOLOS FALL INTO PLAN 3--- (VOCAL 1ST CHORUS, THEN ORCHESTRA, AND FINISHING OFF WITH VOCAL AGAIN)

NOW THAT YOU HAVE THE PLAN CHOSEN START YOUR SKETCH; LEAVING SPACE TO WRITE THE INTRO IN LATER.

   A TWO LINE SKETCH IS SUFFICIENT FOR MOST ARRANGERS. SOME PREFER FOUR LINES (TWO FOR BRASS AND TWO FOR SAXES)

   IT IS NOT NECESSARY TO PUT ALL OF THE RHYTHM PARTS ON YOUR SKETCH. JUST WRITE THEM IN TO REMIND YOURSELF OF ANY SOLO OR SPECIAL EFFECT YOU WANT FROM THEM

BE SURE THE BG SOUNDS GOOD (RHYTHMICALLY, MELODICALLY, HARMONICALLY) BY ITSELF.
   SING IT OUT LOUD OR PLAY IT AND SEE IF IT SOUNDS NATURAL

   THE ENTRANCES OF THE DIFFERENT INSTRUMENTS SHOULD COME IN AT LOGICAL PLACES. (THIS IS RHYTHM ON A LARGER SCALE AGAIN)

   THE HARMONY CHANGES SHOULD HAVE A RHYTHM TOO.
   IE: 1 BAR OF C, 1 BAR OF G MIN.6TH, 2 BARS OF A 9TH, 1 BAR OF D MIN. 7TH, 1 BAR OF G 7TH, 2 BARS OF C; IF YOU TAP OUT THE RHYTHM OF THE HARMONY CHANGES YOU WILL SEE THAT THAT THEY HAVE A RHYTHMIC SIGNIFICANCE OF THEIR OWN.
      THIS EXAMPLE HAPPENS TO HAVE A HARMONIC RHYTHM SIMILAR TO THE RHYTHM OF THE MELODY OF "JINGLE BELLS"

SKETCH THE 1ST CHORUS

   IF 6 OR 8 BARS IN DIFFERENT PARTS OF THE CHORUS ARE IDENTICAL, DON'T WRITE THEM ALL OUT EACH TIME. JUST WRITE, "COPY BARS 5 THROUGH 12" OR WHATEVER BARS THEY HAPPEN TO BE SIMILAR TO. THIS IS CALLED A COME SOPRA (COMB AH SOAP RAH) (THEY SAVE LOTS OF TIME AND EFFORT BUT DO CUT DOWN THE PROFIT IF YOU ARE WORKING BY THE PAGE)

NOW WRITE THE INTRO AND GO AHEAD AND FINISH THE WHOLE SKETCH THEN PUT IT ON SCORE (TRANSPOSED)

BELOW ARE THE PIANO, BASS, GUITAR, AND DRUM PARTS AS THEY WILL LOOK ON THE SCORE.

145.

NOTICE ROOTS AND 5THS ON THE STRONG BEATS OF THE BAR IN THE BASS.

VERY OFTEN THE BASS LINE AND THE NAMES OF THE CHORDS ARE ENOUGH FOR A DANCE BAND PIANIST. THE MELODY IS NECESSARY WHENEVER HE HAS A SOLO.

146.

147.

DRUM PARTS ARE SOMETIMES WRITTEN

148.

GUITAR IS ALWAYS WRITTEN TREBLE CLEF AND SOUNDS AN OCTAVE LOWER THAN WRITTEN.

TRY TO WRITE THE BASS AN INTERESTING PART BUT KEEP HIM CLOSE TO ROOTS AND FIFTHS ON THE MAIN ACCENTS OF THE BAR. HE SOUNDS AN OCTAVE LOWER THAN WRITTEN.

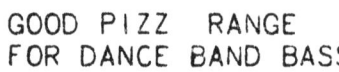

SOME EXAMPLES OF THE USE OF COUNTERPOINT IN DANCE BAND WRITING

A) INDEPENDENT LOWER VOICE (BARITONE SAX, OR BASS SAX, OR BASS CLAR., ETC)

149.

B) INDEPENDENT TOP VOICE

150.

C) CONTRARY MOTION IN THE SAME RHYTHM

151.

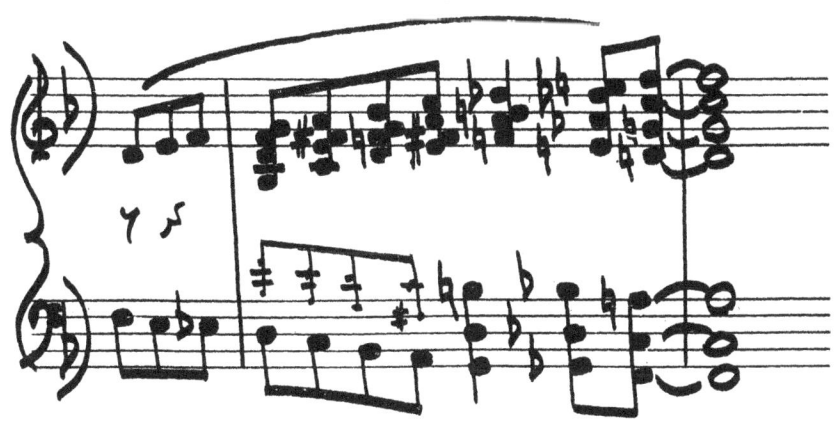

(SEE EX. 318 - 321, HARMONIES RESULTING FROM CONTRAPUNTAL LINES)

153.

CONTRAPUNTAL WRITING OVER THE CHORDAL FRAMEWORK OF A SONG.

154.

155.   156.

AN INCREASE IN TENSION GIVES YOU A NATURAL CRESCENDO

157.
STRINGS ALONE

158
IMITATIONS

ALSO A CANNON STYLE (ROUNDELAY)(SEE EX 300-C) CAN BE USED FOR A SHORT SECTION.

A TWO VOICE INVENTION STYLE IS EFFECTIVE FOR A SHORT PASSAGE IN THE MIDDLE OF AN ARRANGEMENT

WITH CANNON OR INVENTION IT IS USUALLY WISE TO USE JUST DRUMS (NO PIANO, OR GUITAR RHYTHM) IN BACK OF THE COUNTER POINT.

EXAMPLES OF PRESENT DAY DANCE BAND STYLES

BOOK III

SMALL COMBO
  1) PIANO, BASS, GUITAR

159.

        POSSIBILITIES
            ENSEMBLES
            SOLOS
            GUITAR AND PIANO IN 3RDS, OR 6THS, OR 10THS
            GUITAR AGAINST PIANO IN COUNTERPOINT
            BASS CAN ALSO SOLO WITH BG OF PIANO AND GUITAR

A TRIO DOES NOT GIVE YOU MUCH CONTRAST OF COLOR SO THE BEAUTY OF
YOUR ARRANGEMENT WILL DEPEND ON THE PRETTY PHRASES YOU WRITE FOR
THEM, OR THE BEAT, OR THE PHRASING.

NONE OF THE GROUPS OF THIS STYLE ARE USING CLUSTERS YET (SEE EX.90-92)
AS FAR AS I KNOW.

74

2) DIXIELAND COMBO (TWO BEAT)

160.

DIXIELAND STARTED WITH THE JAZZING UP OF SOME OF THE OLD MARCHES, AND STILL HAS MANY OF THE MARCH CHARACTERISTICS SUCH AS:

    A) TWO BEAT RHYTHM

    B) TROMBONE OBLIGATO OR
       TROMBONE ROVING BASS PART

    C) CLARINET ABOVE THE TRPT LEAD

IN THE LAST CHORUS THE TRUMPET USUALLY PLAYS AROUND MELODY WHILE THE CLARINET AND TROMBONE GO WILD AD LIB.

THE PLAN IS USUALLY:

    1ST CHORUS   -   ENSEMBLE

    2ND CHORUS   -   SOLOS (AD LIB)

    3RD CHORUS   -   (4TH, 5TH) MORE SOLOS AD LIB

    LAST CHORUS   -   ENSEMBLE

DIXIE STYLE CAN BE PLAYED WITH A LARGE BAND ALSO BUT SOUNDS MORE CHARACTERISTIC WITH THE SMALL COMBO.

LISTEN TO SOME DIXIE RECORDS AND WRITE A DIXIE ARRANGEMENT

OTHER COMBOS:

    IN SMALL COMBOS OF ANY TYPE THE ARRANGEMENT PLAN IS USUALLY SIMILAR TO THE PLAN ABOVE (FIRST AND LAST CHORUS ENSEMBLE AND SOLOS IN BETWEEN)

    TRUMPET DOES NOT LIKE TO PLAY A HARMONY PART UNDER SAXES BUT BLENDS WELL UNDER CLARINET, OR UNDER OR OVER TROMBONE
    SAXES PLAYING HARMONY UNDER A BRASS INSTRUMENT WORKS WELL.

ENSEMBLE FOR TRPT, ALTO SAX, TENOR SAX, TROMBONE, (& RHYTHM SECTION)

161.   162.

WRITE AN ARRANGEMENT FOR A COMBO OF 4 INSTRUMENTS PLUS RHYTHM SECTION.

76

NOTICE THAT HARMONY TENOR SAXES (2ND & 3RD) ARE:
  SOMETIMES BOTH ABOVE LEAD TENOR
  SOMETIMES ONE ABOVE AND ONE BELOW
  SOMETIMES BOTH BELOW

THE TENORS ARE WRITTEN SO THAT THEY SOUND GOOD AS A SECTION BY THEMSELVES.

IF YOU HAVE A BRASS SECTION WRITE FOR IT IN THE USUAL MANNER (EX.127,128)

IF YOU HAVE FOUR TENORS WRITE THE SAME AS FOR THREE BUT USE FOUR PART HARMONY.

  SOME OF THE POSSIBILITIES FOR 3 TENORS, TRPT AND RHYTHM ARE:

        ENSEMBLE (EX.164)
        TRPT LEAD IN HAT, TENORS PLAYING HARMONY PARTS
        TRPT SOLO - SAXES BG
        PIANO SOLO - SAXES BG
        SAXES - NO BG OR TRPT BG

  IF YOU ADD 3 VIOLINS TO THE ABOVE COMBINATION, WE CAN ALSO HAVE:

        SAXES LEAD - VIOLINS BG
        VIOLINS LEAD - SAXES BG OR NO BG
        (UNISON OR HARM)- (UNISON OR HARM)
        TRPT SOLO - VIOLINS BG
        PIANO SOLO - VIOLINS BG
        VIOLINS LEAD - SAX GOOP - TRPT FILLS

LISTEN ANALYTICALLY TO A TENOR BAND.   WRITE AN ARR. (KEEP IT MOSTLY ENS.)

A COMMERCIAL PIANO PART
(FOR PUBLISHER)
  MUST BE SIMPLE ENOUGH FOR GRANDMA POTTS OUT IN PUMPKIN CENTER, IOWA,
   TO PLAY, AND YET MUST BE COMPLETE RHYTHMICALLY AND HARMONICALLY.

165.

166.

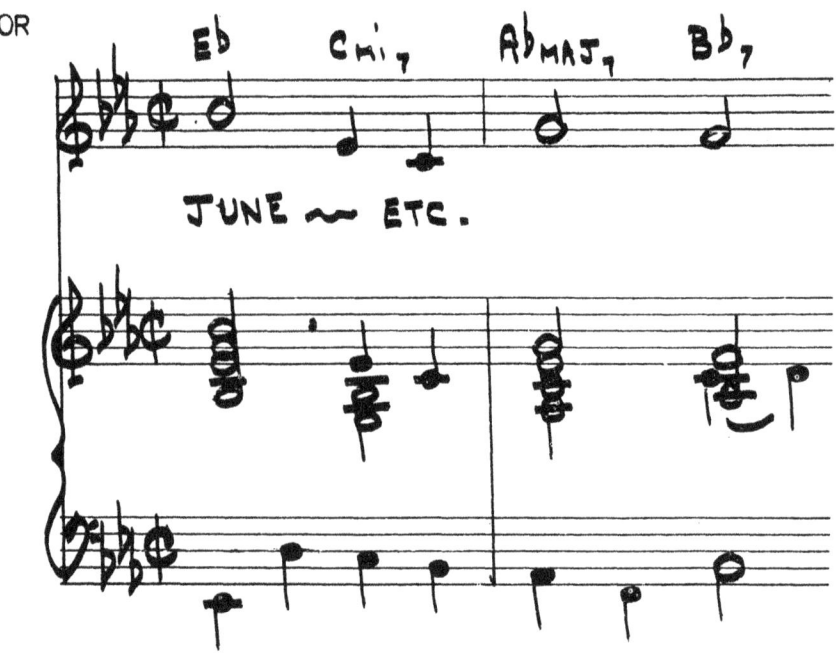

167.

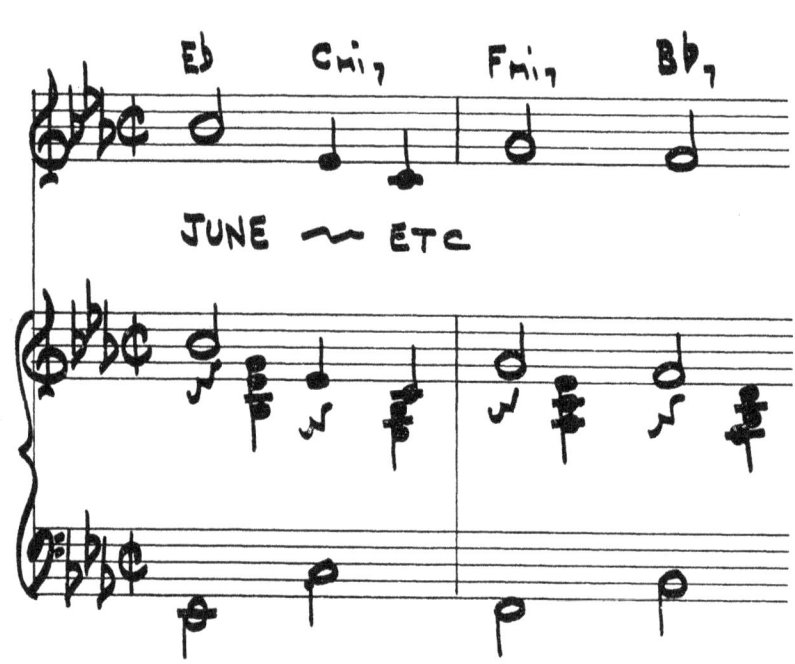

168.

STUDY SOME COMMERCIAL PIANO PARTS AND WRITE ONE ON SOME ORIGINAL TUNE.

STOCK ORCHESTRATIONS AND ARRANGEMENTS FOR VAUDEVILLE ACTS MUST BE WRITTEN SO AS TO SOUND WITH LARGE OR SMALL ORCHESTRA.

WRITE THREE PART HARMONY FOR ALTO 1, ALTO 3, AND TENOR 2, AND GIVE THE TENOR 4 THE EXTRA NOTES (6THS & 9THS ETC.)

169.

DO THE SAME FOR TRPT 1 & 2, AND TROM., AND GIVE THE 3RD TRPT THE LEFTOVER NOTES.

170.

ANOTHER INSURANCE OF A FULL ENSEMBLE IS TO OVERLAP THE BRASS AND SAXES,

171.

THEN YOU WILL HAVE A COMPLETE SOUND WITH SMALL OR LARGE ORCHESTRA.

IN STOCKS THE PLAN IS USUALLY:

    1ST CHORUS
        ENSEMBLE 16 BARS
        SAXES 8 BARS
        ENSEMBLE 16 BARS

    2ND CHORUS
        SAXES 16 BARS
        BRASS OR ENSEMBLE 8 BARS
        SAXES 8 BARS

    MODULATE TO A KEY MORE SUITABLE FOR VOCALISTS
    (DOWN A 4TH OR 5TH)

    3RD CHORUS (VARIETY)
        SOLOS WITH BG OR DIFFERENT COLORS
        (SUCH AS CLARS, MUTED BRASS, ETC.)

    MODULATE TO A HIGHER KEY

    LAST CHORUS (VERY OFTEN JUST 16 BARS AND OUT)
        ENSEMBLE

IN THE PRINTED PARTS THE 1ST AND 2ND CHORUS ARE WRITTEN ON A
DOUBLE STAFF   THIS ENABLES A BAND THAT CUTS UP A STOCK TO USE
ENSEMBLE WHERE THEY WANT IT, OR SAXES, OR BRASS   IE: IF YOU WANT
THE WHOLE CHORUS ENSEMBLE THE BAND CAN PLAY THE TOP LINE ON THE 1ST
16 BARS, THEN THE LOWER LINE FOR THE BRIDGE, AND BACK TO THE TOP LINE
FOR THE LAST 8.

SOME BANDS HAVE THEIR ARRANGER WRITE AN INTRO THEN PLAY TWO CHORUS
(FROM THE 1ST TWO CHORUS OF THE STOCK CUT UP) THEN A WRITTEN MODULATION
TO THE STOCK LAST CHORUS AND POSSIBLY A WRITTEN ENDING. THIS IS NEVER
AS NICE AS A COMPLETE SPECIAL ARRANGEMENT BUT SOMETIMES NECESSARY.
(THIS TYPE OF ARR. GIVES A STOCK A LITTLE INDIVIDUALITY)

VOCAL GROUPS:
FOUR VOICES

172
    (ACTUAL SOUND)

MOST TENORS ARE USED TO READING ONE OCTAVE HIGHER THAN ACTUAL SOUND AND WRITTEN IN TREBLE CLEF.
  IE: THE 2ND VOICE OF EX.172 WOULD BE WRITTEN:

173.

    POSSIBILITIES
        ENSEMBLE
        SOLO WITH BG
        UNISON
        BARBER SHOP OR HYMNAL STYLE

    WITH AN ORCHESTRA YOU CAN ALSO USE THE VOICES JUST LIKE A GROUP
    OF INSTRUMENTS (LIKE ANOTHER SECTION)
        OOO - IS A NICE SYLLABLE FOR A SOFT PASSAGE
        AW OR AH - IS A GOOD SYLLABLE FOR A LOUD SOUND
        HUMMING IS EFFECTIVE

    IF YOU HAVE FIVE VOICES YOU CAN:
        DOUBLE MELODY IN OCTAVES
        OR PUT 5TH VOICE ON ROOTS
        OR USE BIG SPREAD VOICINGS
        (SEE WRITING FOR 5 BRASS, PAGE 26)

SOME EFFECTIVE DEVICES ARE:
  EXAGGERATED EXPRESSION
174.

    SUDDEN CUT OFFS
175.

SUDDEN CUT OFFS LEAVING ONE VOICE HANGING

176.

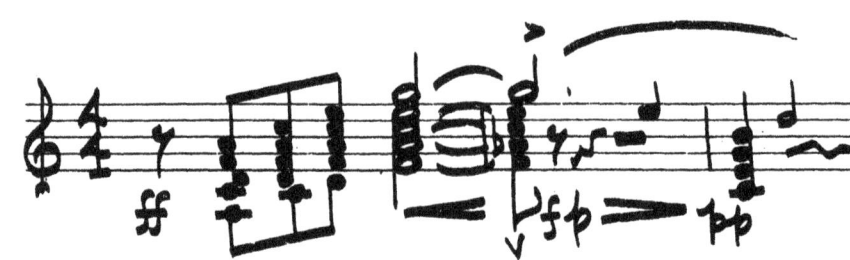

CRESCENDO INTO AN ACCENTED NOTE AND CHANGING SYLLABLE

177.

HIGH OBLIGATOS
(SOPRANO SOUNDING LIKE A THERAMIN OR A MUSICAL SAW)

FUNDAMENTALLY WRITING FOR VOICES IS THE SAME AS WRITING FOR INSTRU-
MENTS EXCEPT VOCAL PARTS HAVE TO HAVE EASY TO SING INTERVALS AND
GOOD NATURAL VOICE LEADING.

IN LARGER VOCAL GROUPS IT IS POSSIBLE TO USE GIRLS AS ONE SECTION
OF INSTRUMENTS AND FELLOWS AS ANOTHER SECTION. THIS WAY YOU CAN
WRITE JUST LIKE YOU WOULD FOR ORCHESTRA. UNISONS, SOLOS, SECTIONS,
BACKGROUNDS. (SEE EX. 127 TO 144 ON POSSIBILITIES OF ORCH.)

WRITE AN ARRANGEMENT FOR A VOCAL GROUP AND HEAR IT PERFORMED.

LARGER ORCHESTRAS

   A) 4 TRUMPETS
      4 TROMBONES
      5 SAXES
      4 RHYTHM

WE CAN USE THE 8 BRASS AS ONE SECTION OR THE TRPTS AND TROMS CAN BE
USED AS SEPARATE SECTIONS

178.

179.
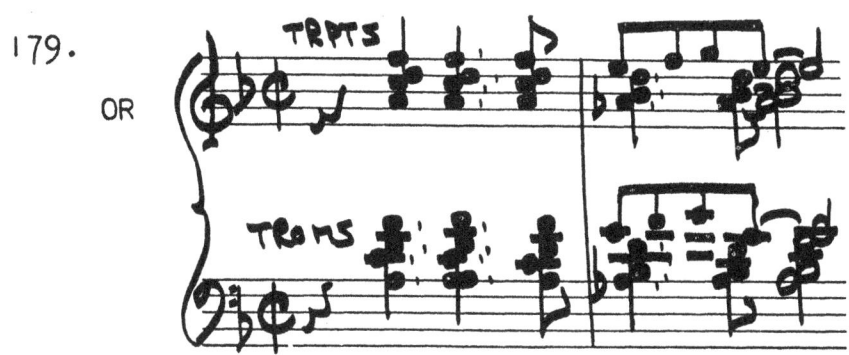

180.
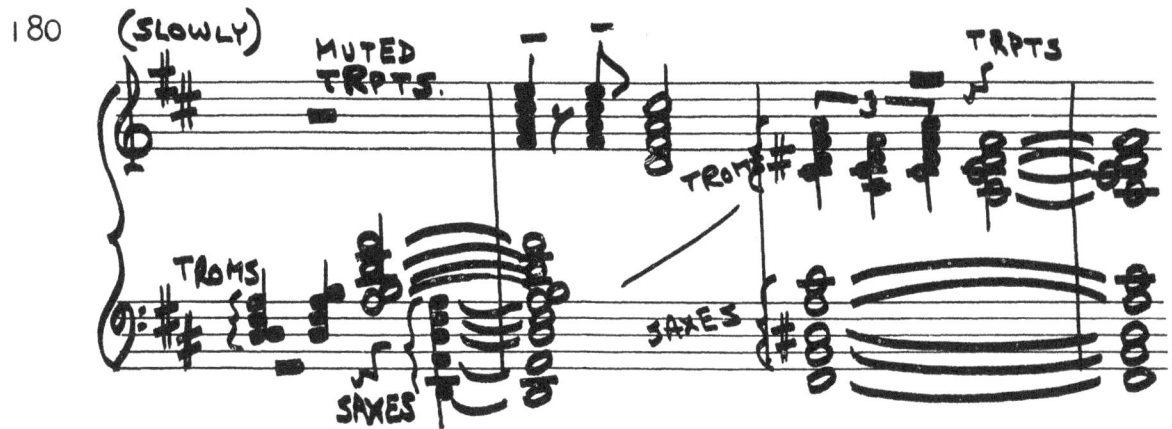

181.

CLUSTERS TIGHT OR SPREAD CAN BE USED WITH THIS TYPE ORCHESTRA ALSO

182
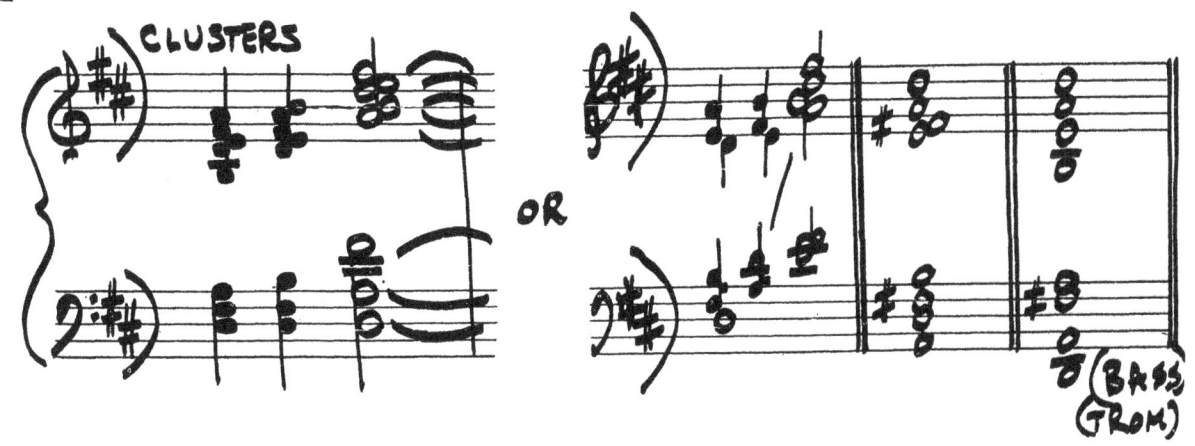

FIGURE OUT HOW MANY MORE ORCHESTRATION POSSIBILITIES YOU CAN USE
(SEE EX. 127 TO 144) WITH THIS SIZE ORCHESTRA.

        ENSEMBLES
        SECTIONS - LEAD
        SOLOS   - BACKGROUND
        UNISONS

LISTEN TO SEVERAL LARGE BAND ARRANGEMENTS AND WRITE AN ARRANGEMENT
FOR THIS COMBINATION.
  GOOD CLEAN TRANSPARENT ORCHESTRATION IS DESIRABLE.
  LET EACH SECTION OR COLOR HAVE ITS OWN PERSONALITY. (SEE 127 TO 144)

STRINGS

A GOOD KNOWLEDGE OF COUNTERPOINT IS A GREAT HELP IN WRITING FOR STRINGS.

  WITH 3 OR 4 STRINGS IN A DANCE BAND WRITE JUST LIKE ANY OTHER
SECTION (TIGHT BLOCK, OR SPREAD, OR UNISON)

  WITH 3 VIOLINS, VIOLA, AND CELLO
  WE CAN WRITE:
      1) BLOCK OR OPEN (JUST AS WE DO WITH BRASS OR SAXES)
      2) 4 PART HARMONY WITH CELLO OBLIGATO
      3) SOLO (VIOLIN, VIOLA, OR CELLO) WITH BG OF THE OTHERS
      4) IN A CONTRAPUNTAL STYLE (IF THERE ARE MORE THAN TWO
         INDEPENDENT VOICES MOVING DON'T USE A RHYTHM SECTION
         WITH IT OR IT WILL SOUND LIKE RHUBARB!)

PEOPLE CAN ONLY HEAR TWO IMPORTANT LINES BESIDES THE RHYTHM SECTION
EXCEPT IN EXTREME CASES.
  ONE EXCEPTION IS WHEN THE EXCITEMENT HAS BUILT TO AN EXTREME PITCH.
ANOTHER IS WHEN THE VOICES ARE ADDED ONE BY ONE, ESPECIALLY ON
REPETITIOUS FIGURES THAT WE TAKE FOR GRANTED AFTER THEY ARE STATED
ONCE OR TWICE. (THEN WE JUST LISTEN TO THE NEW SECTION OR LINE
ENTERING AND IGNORE THE REPEATED FIGURE OR LINE THOUGH ALWAYS
REALIZING THAT IT IS THERE.)
  THE OTHER EXCEPTION IS A BIG FLURRY (BISBIGLIANDO) WHICH IS AN EFFECT
WHERE WE WANT A BIG CONFUSED SOUND. (STRGS RUNNING ARPEGGIOS,
WOODWINDS TRILLING, HARPS GLISSANDOING, CELESTE AND VIBRAPHONE
RUNNING SCALES, BRASS HOLDING BIG CHORDS, AND MAYBE A BIG SMOOTH
FOUR FRENCH HORN UNISON MELODY AGAINST IT ALL)
  A SIMILE IN DRAMA IS THE USE OF CROWD NOISE WHERE NO DISTINCT
DIALOGUE IS HEARD, JUST THE OVERALL EFFECT. IN RADIO OR TV THIS IS
ACHIEVED BY HAVING 4 OR 5 PEOPLE OFF TO THE SIDE, SAYING, "RHUBARB,
RHUBARB, RHUBARB, RHUBARB," (NOT TOGETHER OF COURSE) THIS IS WHERE
CONFUSED COUNTER POINT WITH TOO MUCH GOING ON AT ONCE ACQUIRED ITS
NICKNAME OF "RHUBARB COUNTERPOINT."

SOME OF THE MOST USED EFFECTS IN STRINGS:

DOUBLE STOPS
ANY INTERVAL OF AN OCTAVE OR LESS
6THS, 7THS, 3RDS, AND 2NDS ARE EASILY PLAYED IN TUNE.
8VES, 5THS, AND 4THS ARE USABLE IN PASSAGES THAT DON'T MOVE TOO FAST.

183.
2ND VLN & VIOLA ARE SANDWICHED BECAUSE 7THS ARE MORE EASILY PLAYED THAN 4THS.

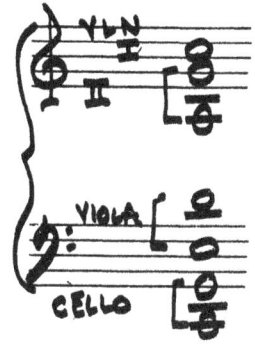

POSSIBLE HARMONICS

184. ANY NOTE ABOVE G ON TOP OF THE TREBLE STAFF MAY BE PLAYED AS A HARMONIC.

A) NATURAL HARMONICS
185.

B) ARTIFICIAL HARMONICS
186.

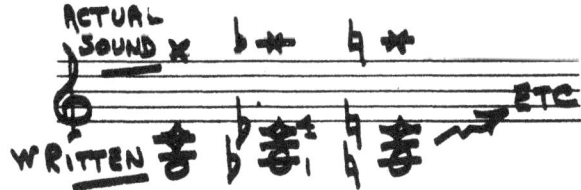

BOWING

UP BOW (∨)
DOWN BOW (⊓)

THE BOWING IN VIOLIN, AND ALL STRING PARTS MUST BE CAREFULLY MARKED. THE FIRST BEAT OF A BAR HAVING A HEAVIER ACCENT THAN THE OTHER BEATS IS USUALLY A DOWN BOW. A VIOLINIST WILL USE A SEPARATE BOW ON EACH NOTE UNLESS IT IS SLURRED OR TIED, SO YOU MUST WRITE IN THE SLURS IF YOU WANT A PASSAGE PLAYED SMOOTHLY.

187.

TIP OF BOW WILL GIVE YOU A LIGHT SOUND. SOFT BECAUSE THEY CANNOT PRESS THE BOW AGAINST THE STRING WITH AS MUCH FORCE.
HEEL OF BOW WILL GIVE YOU A HEAVIER QUALITY.

188.

DOWN BOWS ONE AFTER ANOTHER WILL GIVE YOU A HEAVY ACCENT ON EACH NOTE BECAUSE THEY MUST LIFT THE BOW OFF OF THE STRING TO START EACH NEW DOWN BOW, THEY WILL NECESSARILY GIVE YOU A SEPARATION BETWEEN NOTES.

189.

UP BOWS ONE AFTER ANOTHER GIVE A BUILD UP ON A PHRASE LIKE THIS.

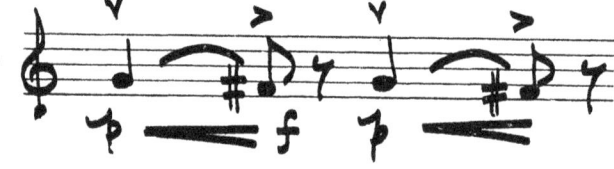

190.

LOURE IS A GROUP OF NOTES PLAYED ON THE SAME BOW WITH A SLIGHT SEPARATION BETWEEN EACH. A LIGHT VIOLINISTIC SOUND

191.

TREMOLO - UP AND DOWN BOWS AS RAPIDLY AS POSSIBLE ON ANY NOTE CAN SOUND SOFT AND ETHEREAL OR LOUD AND DRAMATIC; DON'T USE IT TO EXCESS.

BY THE BRIDGE (PONTICELLO)
  BOWING RIGHT CLOSE TO THE BRIDGE GIVES A THIN GLASSY SOUND

OVER THE FINGERBOARD (SUL TASTO)
  BOWING NEAR THE MIDDLE OF THE STRING GIVES A NASAL QUALITY

LONG BOWS (DÉTACHÉ)
  PULLING AS MUCH AS POSSIBLE THROUGH THE DURATION OF A NOTE

192.

SPICCATO
  BOUNCING THE BOW ON THE STRING FOR A LIGHT FAST STACCATO

193.

JETÉ
  BOUNCING A GROUP OF NOTES ON EITHER AN UP BOW OR A DOWN BOW.

194.

195.   196.

  TRILLS   SHAKES

COL LEGNO
  BOWING WITH THE WOODEN SIDE OF THE BOW INSTEAD OF THE HAIR.
  (BEST FOR LITTLE BOUNCING RHYTHMS.)

197.

"ARCO" MEANS NORMAL BOWING (WHICH, BY THE WAY, SOUNDS VERY NICE)

SLIDE (PORTAMENTO)

198.
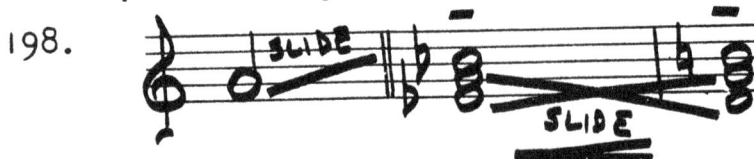

MUTE (SORDINES.) CAN BE USED TO GOOD EFFECT.

SUL G
  MEANS ALL ON G (LOWEST) STRING
 (SUL A, SUL D, SUL E CAN ALSO BE NOTATED)

199.

VIOLINS ARE MORE AT HOME AND SOUND MORE BRILLIANT IN THE SHARP KEYS,
THOUGH ALL GOOD VIOLINISTS CAN PLAY IN ANY KEY WITH FACILITY.

ANYTHING CAN BE PLAYED ON A VIOLIN WITHOUT GIVING TOO MUCH TROUBLE
EXCEPT FAST PASSAGES FULL OF FOURTHS AND FIFTHS. YOU CAN WRITE
SCALES, ARPEGGIOS, CHROMATICS, SKIPS. IT'S PRETTY HARD TO STOP A
GOOD FIDDLE PLAYER.

MANY EFFECTS CAN BE COMBINED
   IE: TIP OF BOW TREMOLO PONTICELLO OR
        HARMONICS TREMOLO
   SEE IF YOU CAN FIND SOME EFFECTS BY COMBINING.

PLEASE USE THESE EFFECTS SPARINGLY. THE VIOLIN STILL SOUNDS WONDERFUL
WHEN PLAYING IN ITS NORMAL NATURAL LEGATO. EFFECTS ARE MOST USEFUL
IN INTROS, MODULATIONS, INTERLUDES, AND ENDINGS. MOST EFFECTS IN
STRINGS SOUND BEST WHEN THE RHYTHM SECTION IS TACIT.

SOME EXAMPLES OF STRING WRITING:
   BLOCK STYLE
200.
   ALSO 2ND VOICE
   CAN BE PULLED
   DOWN AN OCTAVE
   WITH CELLO LEAD
   2 OCTAVES BELOW VIOLIN I

SPREAD OUT

201.

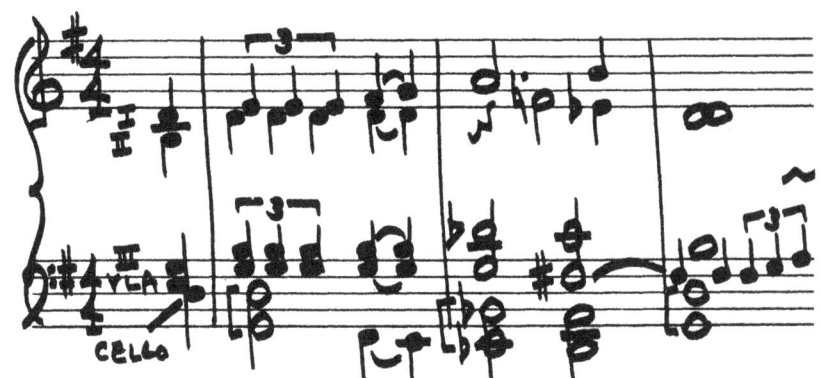

SOLO WITH BACKGROUND

202.

ANOTHER SOLO WITH BACKGROUND

203.

TRY THIS MELODY OR ONE OF YOUR OWN, AND SKETCH IT FOR STRINGS USING SOME OF THE OTHER EFFECTS (SEE EX. 183 TO 199)

ORCHESTRATE A POP TUNE (BALLAD) FOR THREE VIOLINS, VIOLA, AND CELLO. (NO RHYTHM SECTION) NOTICE THAT EX. 201 TO 203 THE RHYTHM IS COMPLETE. (WE FEEL FOUR BEATS IN EACH BAR) THE HARMONY IS COMPLETE. WE NEED NOTHING BUT THE STRINGS ALONE.

THE EXAMPLE BELOW IS A LUSH COMBINATION THAT RECORDS BEAUTIFULLY. STRINGS, CLARS, FRENCH HORN, GUITAR AND BASS FOR RHYTHM SECTION.

204.

IN LARGER ORCHESTRAS (BRASS, REEDS, STRINGS, AND RHYTHM) THE STRINGS CAN BE USED BY THEMSELVES, OR ON LEAD WITH A BG OF ANOTHER COLOR, OR THE STRINGS CAN PLAY BG TO ANY SOLO, OR STRINGS CAN PLAY A UNISON COUNTERPOINT AGAINST AN ENSEMBLE OR ANOTHER SECTION. (IT'S ADVISABLE TO WRITE A COUNTER MELODY IN 3 OR 4 OCTAVE UNISON IF YOU WANT IT TO CUT THROUGH BRASS.)

LISTEN TO SOME LARGE RADIO OR RECORDING ORCHESTRAS AND WRITE A BIG PRODUCTION ARRANGEMENT FOR THIS SIZE ORCHESTRA.

LATIN MUSIC

WHAT WE CALL LATIN MUSIC HAS COME TO AMERICA FROM CUBA, SEVERAL COUNTRIES IN SOUTH AMERICA, AFRICA, AND WHO KNOWS WHERE ELSE.

IT HAS BECOME SO AMERICANIZED THAT IT IS DIFFICULT NOW TO GIVE ANY SET RHYTHMS. THEY ARE PLAYED IN AS MANY DIFFERENT WAYS AS THERE ARE ORCHESTRAS. EVERY DRUMMER SEEMS TO HAVE A SLIGHTLY DIFFERENT CONCEPTION OF THE MANY LATIN RHYTHMS.

THE FOLLOWING PAGES WILL GIVE YOU SOME OF THE MORE POPULAR RHYTHMS AND ALSO HELP YOU TO MAKE UP YOUR OWN. THIS TYPE OF MUSIC IS VERY EXCITING AND ALL TYPES OF MELODY,(PROGRESSIVE, LEGITIMATE, STRAIGHT EIGHTHS, SMOOTH BALLADS, OR EVEN BOOGIE WOOGIE) FIT WELL AND NATURALLY OVER ITS RHYTHM.

A SMALL NUMBER OF PLAYING INSTRUMENTS (POSSIBLY 2 TRPTS, A FEW SAXES, OR VIOLIN, OR FLUTE) WITH AS MANY RHYTHM INSTRUMENTS AS POSSIBLE HAS THE MOST AUTHENTIC SOUND

THIS TYPE OF MUSIC IS ALSO BEAUTIFUL AND EXCITING WHEN PLAYED WITH LARGE ORCHESTRA. (STRINGS, BRASS, HORNS, WOODWIND, RHYTHM)

RHUMBA

THE BASIC BEAT IN ALL RHUMBA IS CALLED THE CLAVE BEAT

THE MARACAS CAN PLAY

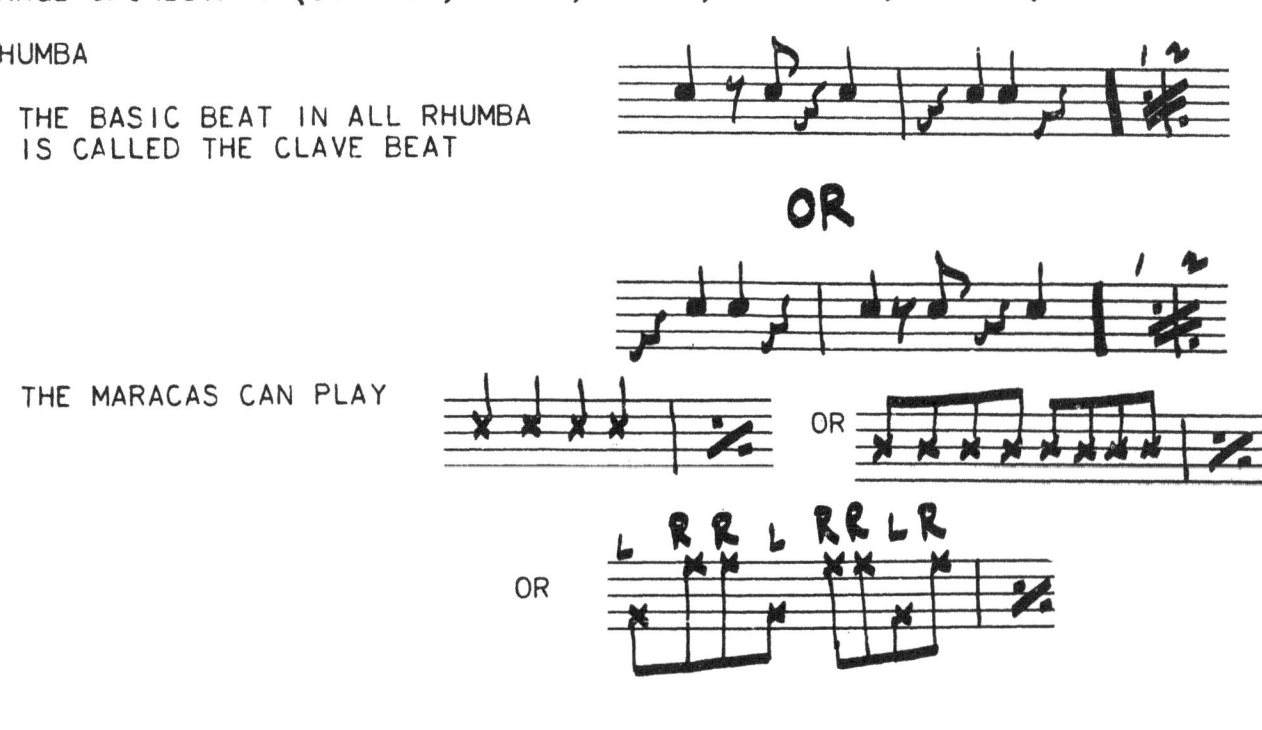

A GOOD RHYTHM FOR GOURD IS

THE DRUMS, BONGOES, TIMBALES, AND GONGA DRUMS USUALLY PLAY WHAT THEY PLEASE, BUT IT SHOULD BE SOME VARIATION OF THE CLAVE BEAT.

IF YOU WANT TO WRITE A RHYTHM FOR THE DRUMS HERE ARE SOME BASIC ONES.

ON A RHUMBA THE PIANO MAY PLAY

205.

CLAVE BEAT

206.

207.

GUARACHA

208.

209.

210.

SAMBA

SAMBA

211. PIANO MAY PLAY

212. OR

DRUM

OR

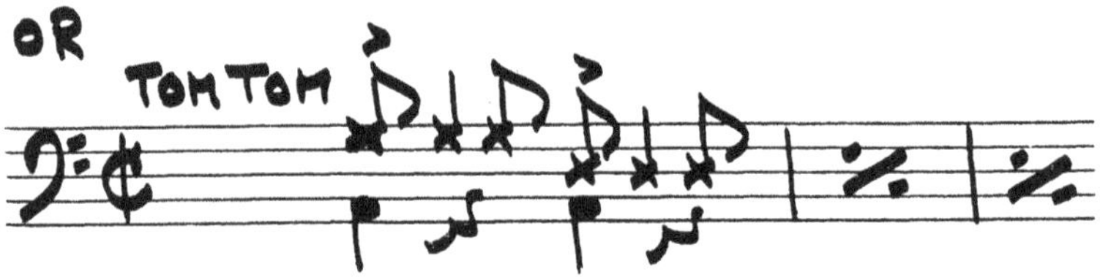

BOTH MARACAS TOGETHER

FORWARD — BACK —

TUBE WITH ONE END FULL OF SHOT

BEGUINE

213.

DRUMS CAN PLAY   OR REGULAR RHUMBA RHYTHM AGAINST THE BEGUINE IS USUALLY MORE EFFECTIVE.

CONGA

214. MOD. FAST

TANGO

215.

THE OLD SPANISH TANGO - VERY SELDOM USED.

216.

PASA DOBLE

217.

FAST DANCES

218. 219.
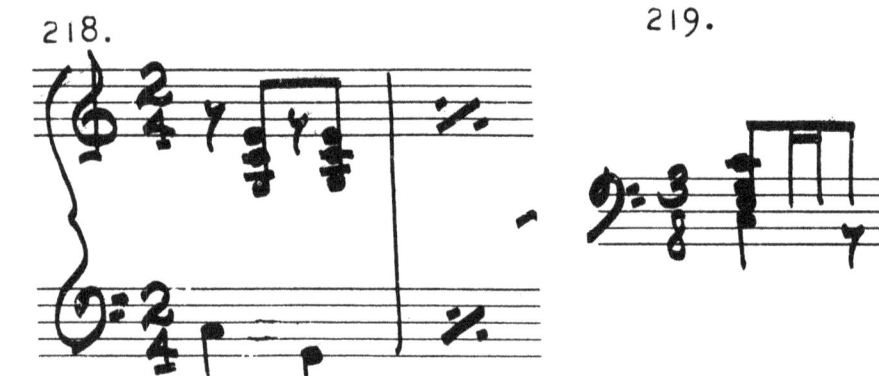

AFRO CUBAN
USUALLY SLOW, VERY SIMILAR TO THE BOLERO ♫♫♫ ♫♫♫ WITH A FEELING OF STRAIGHT 1/8 NOTES, BUT THE AFRO CUBAN HAS MORE ACCENTS.

220.

OR MAKE UP SOME LIKE THE FOLLOWING EXAMPLES

221.

3 DRUMS

222. OR

223. OR

224.   225.

THE GUICA IS EFFECTIVELY USED IN THESE DANCES
A DRUM WITH A ROD PULLED THROUGH IT- HAS A WAILING SOUND

226.

MAMBO
MAMBOS HAVE THE FEEL OF THE REVERSED CLAVE BEAT.

MAMBOS ARE LIKE RIFF TUNES; REPEATED RHYTHM PATTERNS, USUALLY
4 BARS OR 8 BARS CAN BE 2, OR POSSIBLY 5, OR ETC. OFTEN ONE RHYTHM
PATTERN IS STARTED AND AS IT IS REPEATED ANOTHER IS ADDED AGAINST IT
THEN ANOTHER IS ADDED AND SO ON; THESE CAN BE WRITTEN AS ONE
COUNTERPOINT AGAINST ANOTHER AND SO ON, OR AS A CHORD PATTERN WITH
DIFFERENT RHYTHMS SUPERIMPOSED ON EACH OTHER ADDED ONE BY ONE.

MAMBOS ARE VERY EXCITING. THEY USUALLY START SOFT AND BUILD AND BUILD AND THEN DROP BACK SOFT AGAIN. SOMETIMES THEY BUILD UP A SECOND TIME HITTING A BIGGER CLIMAX QUICKER AND THEN DROP BACK TO A SOFT FINISH. AT THE CLIMAX A WILD AD LIB CAN BE ADDED ON TOP OF EVERYTHING.

AN ARRANGEMENT CAN BE COMPLETELY MAMBO FROM BEGINNING TO END, OR IN THE MIDDLE OF A REGULAR RHUMBA OR GUARACHA WE CAN HAVE AN AD LIB SOLO OVER A PERSISTENT FIGURE A LA MAMBO.

IE: AFTER 2ND CHORUS.

OFTEN A BACKGROUND FIGURE IS PLAYED TWICE THEN AN AD LIB SOLO COMES IN ON TOP OF IT AS IT CONTINUES TO REPEAT. IT SHOULD BUILD AND BUILD AND AT A GIVEN SIGNAL (A LIP TRILL OR GROWL OR FLUTTER TONGUE FOR 4 BARS CAN BE USED) THE WHOLE ENSEMBLE, CRASHES INTO THE LAST CHORUS.

PLAN:
2 CHORUS OF RHUMBA
MAMBO
RHUMBA LAST CHORUS   POSSIBLY IN A HIGHER KEY

A MAMBO OVER A DOMINANT 7TH TYPE HARMONY HAS A VERY DISTINCTIVE FLAVOR.

MONTUNO

AN AD LIB SOLO WITH JUST RHYTHM INSTRUMENTS PLAYING IN BACK OF IT.

HAVING NO HARMONIES IN THE BACKGROUND GIVES THE SOLO COMPLETE FREEDOM TO PLAY ANY HARMONIES OR IN ANY KEY HE WANTS TO, AS LONG AS HE FINALLY WORKS BACK TO THE KEY THE ORCHESTRA IS GOING INTO AT THE END OF THE MONTUNO.

PIANO, OR TRPT, OR FLUTE, OR CLAR. MONTUNOS ARE VERY EFFECTIVE.

MONTUNOS ARE ALSO MOST EFFECTIVE JUST BEFORE THE LAST CHORUS OF ANY MODERATE OR FAST TEMPO LATIN STYLE ARRANGEMENT.

PLAN:
2 CHORUS
THEN MONTUNO
LAST CHORUS

WRITE A RHUMBA, A MAMBO AND ETC.

EVERY ARRANGER SHOULD KEEP UP ON THE CLICHES OF THE DAY   UNLESS HE WANTS SOMEONE TO ASK HIM IF HE LIKES THE WAY HE WRITES AS WELL AS THE WAY THEY WRITE NOWADAYS

BE ABLE TO WRITE ANY STYLE

ONE CHARACTERISTIC OF OUR DANCE MUSIC NOW IS A VERY RELAXED, LOOSE BUT SOLID BEAT. IT CAN BE FELT SUBTLEY, EVEN IF IT SOMETIMES IS NOT TOO APPARENT   THE RHYTHM SECTION SHOULD BE ABLE TO DROP OUT AT ANY TIME AND THE BAND PLAY RIGHT ON IN THE SAME RELAXED GROOVE.   THIS GIVES THE DRUMMER AND THE RHYTHM SECTION MANY MORE LIBERTIES THAN IF THE BAND IS DEPENDENT ON THEM FOR ITS BEAT

SOME OF THE CLICHES THAT HAVE BEEN POPULAR IN THE LAST FEW YEARS ARE
1) LITTLE TRILLS AND TURNS
   TURNS

2) THE FAMOUS (OR INFAMOUS) FLAT FIFTH

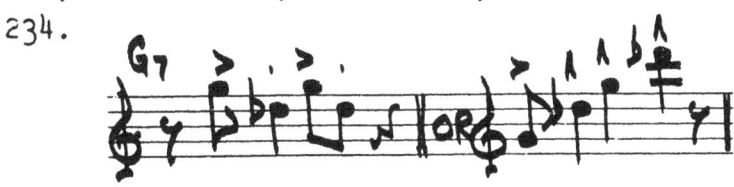

3) NOTES JUST A HALF STEP ABOVE OR BELOW CHORDAL NOTES
IT IS NOT NECESSARY TO RESOLVE THEM.

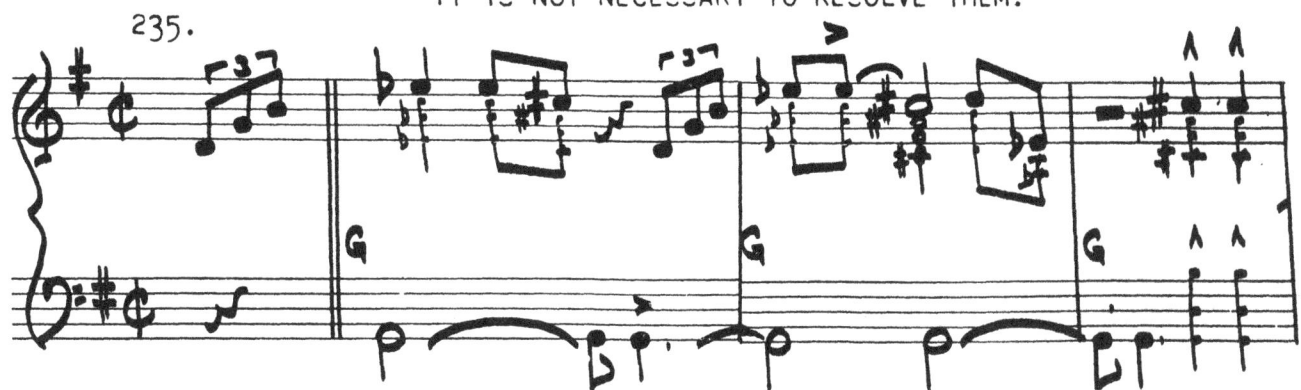

4) TRIPLETS IN THE ORCHESTRATION (THE DRUMS CAN HELP ACCENT THESE)

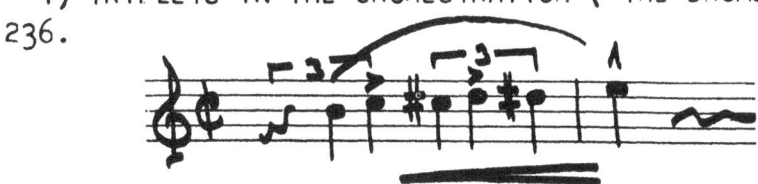

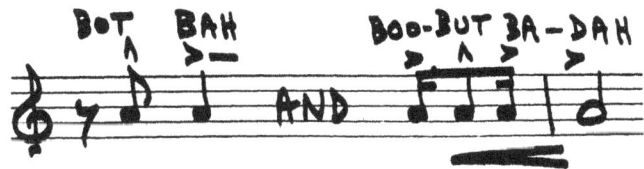

5) VERY STRAIGHT ON THE BEAT FIGURES ACCENTED WITH THE HELP OF THE DRUMMER. THEY CAN SOUND OH SO SQUARE IF THE DRUMMER DOESN'T CATCH THEM.

6) DOUBLE AND TRIPLE TIME FIGURES.

7) HYPER TENSION CHORDS.

8) THE DEAD TONE (NO VIBRATO) IS QUITE POPULAR NOW.

9) FREQUENT USE OF THE PRETTY NOTES AGAINST THE CHORDS, 11THS-13THS-9THS ETC.

SOME OF THE MORE CREATIVE INSTRUMENTALISTS HAVE FOUND THAT IF THEY KEEP VERY STILL AND RELAXED, (COOL) PHYSICALLY WHILE PLAYING, THEY CAN PUT MUCH MORE INTO THEIR SOLOS.

ONE THING THAT HAS HURT THE REPUTATION OF A LOT OF OUR PRESENT DAY DANCE MUSIC IS THE FACT THAT THE YOUNG WORSHIPERS HAVE COPIED MANY OF THE BAD QUALITIES OF THE HEROES OF THE DAY, INSTEAD OF JUST COPYING THE GOOD QUALITIES.

PROGRESSIVE MUSIC

MEANS JUST WHAT THE TITLE IMPLIES, AND EVEN THOUGH A GOOD PORTION OF SO CALLED PROGRESSIVE MUSIC IS NOT IN GOOD TASTE, THAT PORTION OF IT THAT IS WORTHWHILE IS WORTH ALL THE EFFORT. I THINK IT SHOWS A WONDERFULLY HEALTHY ATTITUDE TO NOT BE SATISFIED WITH THE WAY GRANDFATHER DID IT. IT TAKES COURAGE AND I THINK WE SHOULD BOW OUR HEAD EVER SO SLIGHTLY TO ANYONE WHO ADVANCES ANY ART AND TRIES TO EDUCATE THE PEOPLE.

INTRODUCTIONS
MODULATIONS
INTERLUDES
ENDINGS

BOOK IV

INTRODUCTIONS, INTERLUDES, MODULATIONS, AND ENDINGS.

INTROS CAN BE BUILT FROM
1) FRAGMENTS OF THE TUNE (OR A FRAGMENT OF SOME COUNTER MELODY IN YOUR FIRST CHORUS.)
USUALLY IT IS ADVISABLE TO USE THE FRAGMENT OVER DIFFERENT HARMONIES THAN THE EXPECTED (SEE SUBSTITUTE CHORDS, EX.291 TO 297) ESPECIALLY IF YOU USE THE FIRST PART OF YOUR TUNE AS A FRAGMENT.

OR 2) A CHORD PROGRESSION (POSSIBLY SUGGESTED BY SOME HARMONIC CHANGE THAT IS OUTSTANDING IN YOUR FIRST CHORUS)

OR 3) COMPLETELY UNRELATED MATERIAL (USUALLY IN THE SAME GENERAL STYLE AS YOUR TUNE) READ THE LYRICS OF THE SONG AND SEE WHAT MOOD THEY SUGGEST. (IF YOU USE UNRELATED MATERIAL IN THE INTRO THAT IS OUTSTANDING BE SURE TO REFER TO IT ELSEWHERE IN THE ARRANGEMENT. A LOGICAL PLACE TO USE SOME OF THE SAME MATERIAL IS IN MODULATIONS, INTERLUDES, AND ENDINGS. OR POSSIBLY IN A BACKGROUND COUNTERPOINT.

OR 4) THE RHYTHM PATTERNS THAT ARE USED BEHIND THE MELODY OF THE CHORUS MAY BE ESTABLISHED IN THE INTRO.

238.

TWO OF THE MOST OBVIOUS FRAGMENTS IN EX. 238 ARE

239. AND 240.

ONE POSSIBLE INTRO BUILT FROM THE 1ST FRAGMENT (EX.239) COULD BE

241.

IF FIRST CHORUS IS A SOLO EITHER END THE INTRO FULL AND BIG OR BUILD INTO THE FIRST NOTE OF THE FIRST CHORUS.

IF THE FIRST CHORUS STARTS FULL ENSEMBLE, END THE INTRO. THIN.

THE LISTENER CANNOT TELL WHERE THE INTRO ENDS AND WHERE THE CHORUS STARTS IF THEY ARE BOTH THE SAME COLOR AND LOUDNESS.

A POSSIBLE INTRO OUT OF THE SECOND FRAGMENT OF THE TUNE (EX.240)

242.

AN INTRO BUILT OVER A CHORD STRUCTURE. (SEE ROOT PROG. EX.269) FOR EX. 243 WE HAVE CHOSEN B♭, A♭ 9TH, G♭ 9TH, F 9TH)

NOTICE THE LAST CHORD IN ALMOST EVERY INTRO IS THE DOMINANT 7TH (V 7) CHORD (IN THE KEY THE FIRST CHORUS STARTS IN) OR ITS SUB- STITUTE (THE CHORD BUILT ON THE FLAT FIFTH OF THE DOMINANT.)

IN THE KEY OF B♭, THE DOMINANT 7TH CHORD (THE DOM.7TH CHORD IS ALWAYS BUILT ON THE FIFTH STEP OF THE SCALE) IS F 7TH AND ITS SUB- STITUTE IS C♭ 7TH. SO EITHER F 7TH OR C♭ 7TH LEAD INTO THE KEY OF B♭

PREFERABLY THE MELODY NOTE JUST BEFORE GOING INTO THE CHORUS (THE LAST NOTE OF THE INTRO) IS A STRONG NOTE IN OUR KEY (5TH STEP OF THE SCALE OR 3RD STEP OF THE SCALE) SEE EX.241,242,243. THE LAST NOTE OF THE INTRO MAY BE A NOTE THAT PROGRESSES SMOOTHLY INTO THE FIRST NOTE OF THE CHORUS ALSO.(BY HALF STEP, WHOLE STEP, OR COMMON TONE)

243.

IF A VOCALIST HAS TO ENTER AFTER THE INTRO GIVE (HER - HIM) A GOOD STRONG KEY FEELING. I'VE SEEN CASES WHERE IT WAS NECESSARY TO HAVE SOME STRONG INSTRUMENT PLAY THE VOCALISTS FIRST NOTE AS A BELL TONE TO BRING HER IN, BUT THIS IS ONLY NECESSARY WHEN YOU ARE WRITING FOR A BEAUTIFUL GIRL WHO DOUBLES ON SINGING.

A RHYTHM PATTERN MAY BE USED FOR THE WHOLE INTRO AND THEN CONTINUED ON DURING THE CHORUS AS BACKGROUND FOR THE MELODY, OR YOU MAY WRITE A FOUR (OR 2, OR 6, OR 8, ETC) BAR REGULAR INTRO AND THEN GO INTO FOUR BARS OF THE RHYTHM PATTERN WHICH MAKES AN EIGHT BAR INTRO.

RHYTHM PATTERN INTRO

244.

DON'T LET THE RHYTHM PATTERN BECOME MONOTONOUS.
VARY IT.   (SEE EX. 343, 344)

MODULATIONS
(LEAVING ONE TONALITY (KEY) AND ESTABLISHING ANOTHER)

YOU CAN MODULATE INTO ANY KEY THROUGH ITS DOMINANT 7TH (THE CHORD BUILT ON THE FIFTH STEP OF THE SCALE OF THE NEW KEY) OR ITS SUBSTITUTE (THE CHORD BUILT ON THE FLAT FIFTH OF THE DOMINANT) SEE EX.97.

SIMPLE TWO BAR MODULATION FROM C TO E♭.

245.   OR   246.

FOR A STRONGER MODULATION USE A STRONG ROOT PROGRESSION INTO THE DOM.7TH OF THE NEW KEY (SEE ROOT PROG. EX.269)

247.   FROM D MAJOR
         TO F MAJOR

ALWAYS WORK BACKWARDS FROM THE NEW KEY WHEN LOOKING FOR A CHORD PROGRESSION TO USE.

248.

THE MOST SATISFYING MODULATIONS ARE THOSE WHICH CHANGE TO DISTANTLY RELATED KEYS.

SOME OF THE FRESHEST SOUNDING KEY CHANGES ARE:

UP A HALF STEP	IE	C TO D♭
UP A MIN. 3RD	"	C TO E♭
UP A MAJ. 3RD	"	C TO E
UP AN AUG. 4TH	"	C TO F# OR G♭
UP A MIN. 6TH	"	C TO A♭ (SAME AS DOWN A MAJ.3RD)
UP A MAJ. 6TH	"	C TO A " " " " MIN.3RD)
UP A MIN. 7TH	"	C TO B♭ " " " " MAJ.2ND)
DOWN A MIN. 2ND	"	C TO B

CHANGING KEY FROM C TO F, OR C TO G, OR C TO D,
ARE HARDLY MODULATIONS THE KEYS ARE SO CLOSELY RELATED.

WHEN IT IS NECESSARY TO MODULATE TO A CLOSELY RELATED
KEY, IT IS OFTEN MORE EFFECTIVE TO MODULATE SUDDENLY
TO A DISTANT KEY AND THEN WORK BACK TO THE CLOSELY RELATED
KEY.

SURPRISE MODULATIONS

1) COMMON TONE MODULATIONS ARE MOST EFFECTIVE IF THE NOTE BECOMES
AN ACTIVE NOTE ON THE DOWN BEAT OF THE CHORUS. AN ACTIVE NOTE IS
ANY NOTE THAT IS A MAJ. OR A MIN. 2ND, OR A MAJ. OR A MIN. 7TH
INTERVAL FROM ANOTHER NOTE IN THE CHORD. IN EX. 249 THE B IS
THE ROOT OF THE B 7TH CHORD AND SUDDENLY BECOMES A MAJ. 7TH OF THE
NEXT CHORD, WHICH IS A VERY ACTIVE NOTE. IT IS IMPERATIVE IN
SURPRISE MODULATIONS TO GO TO A REMOTE KEY. THE THIRD OF A MAJOR
CHORD IS ALSO A GOOD NOTE TO BUILD INTO. SOMETIMES THE COMMON
TONE CAN BE IN AN INNER VOICE. (EX.251) ALSO THE MELODY CAN
MOVE UP (OR DOWN) A HALF OR A WHOLE STEP INTO A FRESH NEW KEY.(EX 251)

249.

IN EX. 249, B   IS THE COMMON TONE.

250.

251.

USING INTRO MATERIAL IN MODULATIONS (SAME MATERIAL CAN BE USED IN ENDING ALSO)

MODULATION FROM B♭ TO D♭
(MATERIAL BORROWED FROM INTRO EX.238)

252.

WRITE MODULATIONS FROM
   C TO E♭
   F TO D♭
   D TO B♭   (USE DOM 7THS, SUB DOM. 7THS, SURPRISE MODULATIONS)
   G♭ TO D
   E♭ TO G
   C TO E♭ MIN.

PLAY THE II 7, V 7, I CHORDS IN ALL KEYS (MAJOR & MINOR)

253.

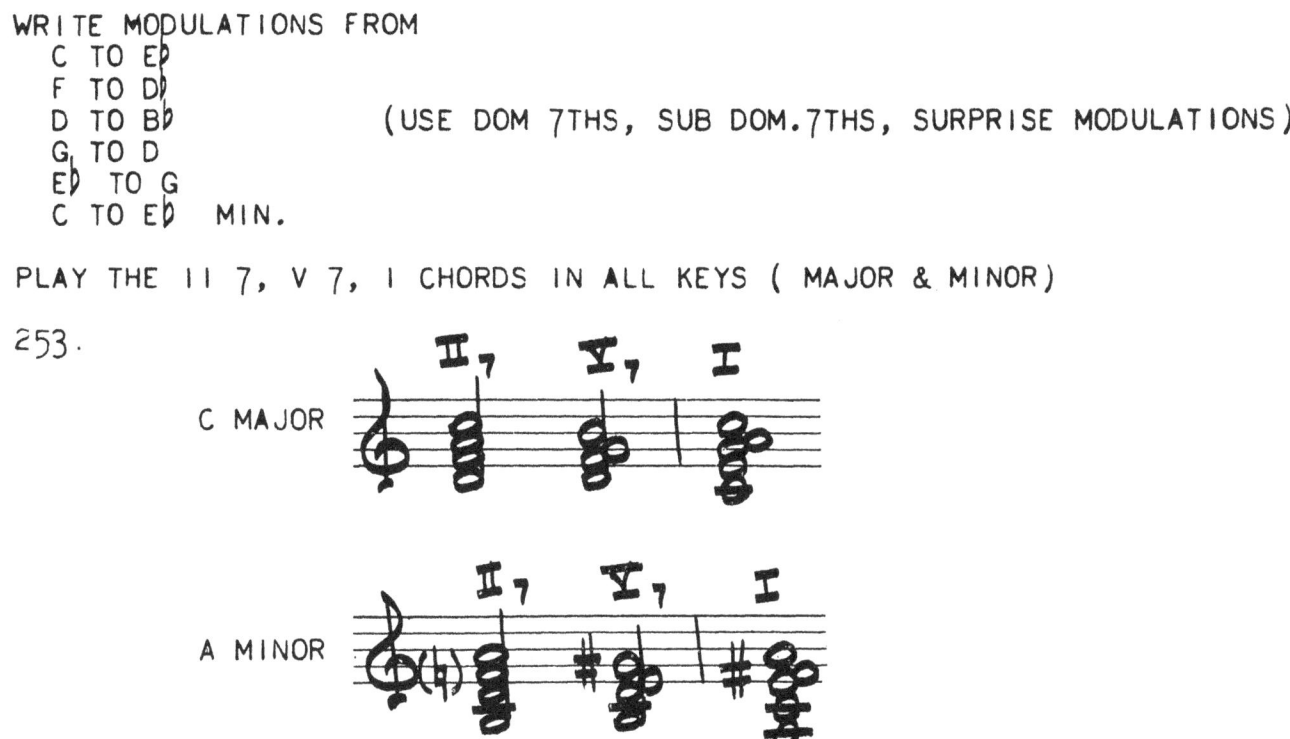

MODULATIONS CAN ALSO BE BUILT OVER A CHORD PROGRESSION
   (EITHER A GOOD ROOT PROGRESSION OR A PARALLEL PROGRESSION)

254.

WRITE A MODULATION OVER THE FOLLOWING PROGRESSIONS

1) ONE BAR EACH OF C, B♭ 9TH, D♭ 9TH, F# 7TH.
2) ONE BAR EACH OF D, F 7TH, A♭ 7TH, G 7TH

EXAMPLE 254 SOUNDS HARMONICALLY CONVINCING BECAUSE OF STRONG ROOT PROGRESSIONS TOWARD THE END OF THE PHRASE. (C ROOT TO A♭ ROOT IS NOT STRONG, A♭ TO G♭ IS FAIRLY STRONG, AND G♭ TO F AND F TO B♭ ARE BOTH VERY STRONG.

ENDINGS

FROM FRAGMENT OF INTRO (EX. 238-240)

255.   OR   256.

257.

ENDING WRITTEN OVER A CHORD PROGRESSION

258.

TRY WRITING AN ENDING OVER THE FOLLOWING PROGRESSIONS;
(FIND SOME PRETTY NOTES AGAINST THE CHORDS)   SEE EX. 115 TO 120)
    G 6TH, F 9TH, G 6TH
    G 6TH, C 9TH, G 6TH
    G 6TH, E♭ 9TH, G 6TH
    G 6TH, A♭ MAJ. 7TH, G 6TH
    G 6TH, E♭ MAJ. 7TH, A♭ MAJ. 7TH, G MAJ. 7TH
        (PLEASE DON'T USE G 6TH, C 6TH, G 6TH)

ENDINGS MAY STAPT OUT JUST LIKE THE CHORUS MELODY AND THEN WORK
INTO FINAL CADENCE.   (TUNE IS EX. 238)

259.

ENDINGS MAY USE A SURPRISE CHORD (DECEPTIVE CADENCE) ON LAST NOTE OF
CHORUS AND THEN RESOLVE INTO FINAL CHORD.   SEE EX. 260.

260.

SURPRISE CHORD MAY TURN BACK INTO LAST PHRASE OF TUNE (EXTENSION)

261.

ANOTHER TYPE OF EXTENSION MAY BE EFFECTED BY AVOIDING THE ROOT OF THE TONIC CHORD IN THE BASS ON THE LAST NOTE OF THE CHORUS AND THEN EXTENDING THE PHRASE.

262.

FOR MORE IDEAS TO EXPERIMENT WITH IN WRITING INTROS SEE BOOK III.

   INTROS, MODULATIONS, INTERLUDES, AND ENDINGS PROVIDE THE MOST OPPORTUNITY FOR THE USE OF SPECIAL EFFECTS. (SEE VLN EFFECTS, EX 183 TO 199) IT IS OFTEN EFFECTIVE TO USE THE RHYTHM SECTION SPARINGLY IN THE INTRO ESPECIALLY ON PRETTY TUNES. THE LINES, HARMONIES, VOICINGS, AND ORCHESTRA COLORS HAVE MORE BEAUTY AND CLARITY IF THE RHYTHM IS NOT PLAYING AS A RHYTHM SECTION.

   BE SURE THAT ANYTHING OUTSTANDING IN YOUR ARRANGEMENT IS NOT REFERRED TO JUST ONCE. (3 IS A GOOD NUMBER) IF A SENSATIONAL OR ATTRACTIVE IDEA OCCURS JUST ONCE IT SOUNDS OUT OF PLACE. (LIKE A BIG BLOTCH OF RED IN A PAINTING OF ALL COOL COLORS THAT ARE UNRELATED TO RED) THIS ALSO HELPS YOU TO BUILD YOUR ARRANGEMENT OUT OF FEWER IDEAS WHICH IS AN IMPORTANT POINT AND A FAILING OF ALMOST ALL BEGINNING ARRANGERS.

WRITE AN ENDING TO ANY POP OR STANDARD TUNE USING A DECEPTIVE CADENCE AND AN EXTENSION.

HARMONIC PROGRESSION
ALTERED CHORDS
SUBSTITUTE CHORDS
MELODY WRITING

BOOK V

LOGICAL HARMONIC PROGRESSION:

ROOT PROGRESSION-FROM THE ROOT (NOT NECESSARILY THE LOWEST NOTE) OF ONE CHORD TO THE NEXT.

TO FIND THE ROOT OF A CHORD LOOK FOR THE STRONGEST INTERVAL IN THE CHORD. LOOK FIRST FOR THE INTERVAL OF A FIFTH (PERF.5TH). IF YOU FIND A PERF.5TH, THE LOWEST NOTE OF THE 5TH WILL BE THE ROOT OF THE CHORD.

IF THERE IS NO PERF.5TH IN THE CHORD, LOOK FOR THE NEXT STRONGEST INTERVAL (SEE EX. 114) WHICH WILL BE A PERF.4TH (THE INVERSION OF A PERF.5TH) THE TOP NOTE OF THIS PERF.4TH WILL BE THE ROOT THEN.

IF THERE IS NO PERF.4TH LOOK FOR THE NEXT STRONGEST INTERVAL IN THE CHORD WHICH WILL BE A MAJ.3RD. OR ITS INVERSION, THE MIN.6TH.

FOLLOWING IS A CHART OF THE INTERVALS IN THE ORDER OF THEIR HARMONIC STRENGTH:

263.

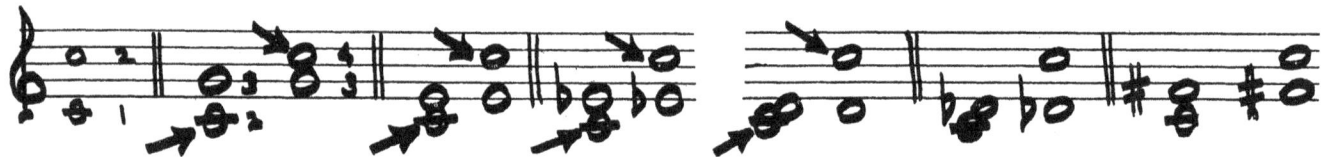

FIND THE ROOTS OF THE FOLLOWING CHORDS:

264

A SUSPENSION IS TREATED AND THOUGHT OF JUST AS IF IT WERE THE NOTE IT IS SUBSTITUTED FOR:

265.

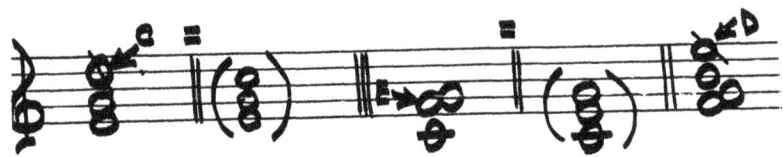

FIND THE ROOTS OF THE FOLLOWING CHORDS:
266.

THE ROOT PROGRESSION OF THE FOLLOWING EXAMPLE IS G TO C (UP A PERF. 4TH)
267.

FIND THE ROOT PROGRESSION OF THE FOLLOWING EXAMPLE:
268.

BELOW ARE LISTED THE ROOT PROGRESSIONS IN THE ORDER OF THEIR STRENGTH:
    1) DOWN A PERF. 5TH (UP A PERF. 4TH)
    2) DOWN A MIN. 2ND
    3) UP A MAJ. 2ND
    4) UP A PERF 5TH
    5) DOWN A MAJ. 2ND
    6) UP A MIN. 2ND.
    ALL THE OTHERS (3RDS, 6THS, ETC.) ARE VERY WEAK ROOT PROG.

269.

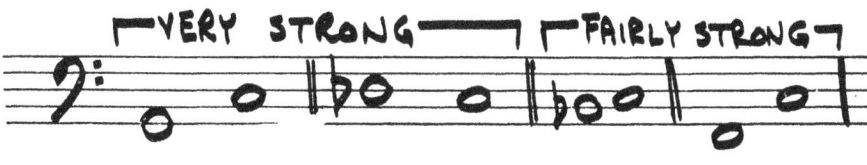

MEMORIZE THE FOUR STRONGEST ROOT PROGRESSIONS.

WHICH OF THE FOLLOWING HAVE STRONG ROOT PROGRESSIONS AND WHICH HAVE WEAK ROOT PROGRESSIONS:

270.

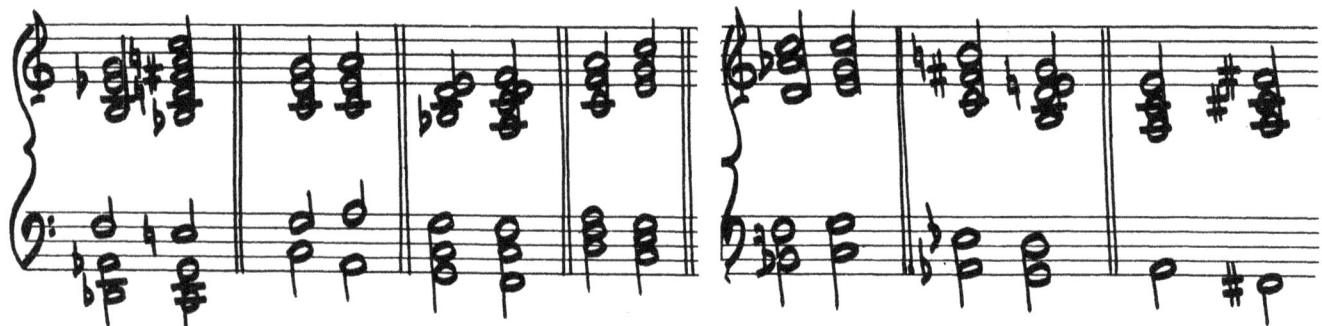

TOWARD THE END OF A PHRASE (OR TOWARD THE END OF A COMPOSITION) A STRONG ROOT PROGRESSION IS DESIREABLE.
ANALYZE THE FOLLOWING ROOT PROGRESSIONS:
THESE WERE CONCEIVED BY WORKING FROM THE END OF THE PHRASE BACK.
IE: G IS THE LAST ROOT IN THE PHRASE,
LOOKING BACK FROM G, EITHER D, A♭ , OR F WILL MAKE A STRONG ROOT PROGRESSION INTO G.   THEN WE CAN LOOK BACK FROM D, A♭ , OR F AND FIND WHAT NOTES WILL MAKE A STRONG ROOT PROGRESSION INTO THEM, ETC. ETC.

AT THE BEGINNING OF A PHRASE WE CAN START WITH A WEAK ROOT PROGRESSION BUT THEN WE MUST START LEADING HOME AGAIN WITH   STRONG PROGRESSIONS.
FROM ONE PHRASE INTO ANOTHER NO RULES APPLY. A PHRASE IS A COMPLETE STATEMENT (EVEN IF IT DOES NOT END FINALLY), AND THE NEXT PHRASE MAY START IN A NEW KEY, OR WITH A WEAK ROOT PROGRESSION , ETC ,

271.

271 (CONTINUED)

NOW PLAY THROUGH THE CYCLE OF KEYS. (UP A 4TH IS THE MOST NATURAL PROG)
(THIS GIVES YOU A FEELING OF MOVING FORWARD)

C TO F TO B♭ TO E♭ TO A♭ TO D♭ TO G♭ (OR F#) TO B TO E TO A TO D TO G AND BACK TO C.

TRY:
272.

NOW DO THE SAME USING THE II7, V7, I CHORDS OF EACH KEY.

273.

NOTICE IN THE ABOVE THE TWO BAR SEQUENCES. (EACH TWO BARS IS SIMILAR TO THE NEXT TWO EXCEPT FOR BEING ON A DIFFERENT PITCH)

NOW GO THROUGH THE CYCLE USING SUBSTITUTE DOMINANTS (BUILT ON THE FLAT FIFTH OF THE DOM.) (G♭ 7TH INSTEAD OF C 7TH)

274.

NOTICE THE ABOVE ARE ONE BAR SEQUENCES.
PLAY THE CYCLE USING ALL DOM 7TH CHORDS (C 7TH, TO F 7TH TO B♭ 7TH, ETC.)
NOW PLAY THE CYCLE USING A DOM. SUBSTITUTE EVERY OTHER CHORD
(C 7TH, TO C♭ 7TH, TO B♭ 7TH, ETC.)
WE CAN ALSO HAVE A CYCLE OF ANY TYPE CHORDS, OR MIXTURES OF DIFFERENT TYPE CHORDS.
ALSO PLAY THROUGH THE CYCLE GOING BACKWARDS ALL THE WAY (UP A 5TH EACH TIME) (C TO G TO D TO A, ETC.)

WE HAVE A CYCLE WITHIN A KEY ALSO:

275.

SOME HARMONIC PROGRESSIONS FOR DIFFERENT STYLE SONGS:
    CYCLE (EX. 277)
    VAMP (EX 283, 277, 278)
    SUDDEN KEY CHANGE AT THE BEGINNING OF A NEW PHRASE (EX.283)
    CHROMATIC (EX 279)
    PARALLELS (EX.285)
    HILL BILLY (EX 288)
    WESTERN (EX.288)
    MINOR MAJOR
    GYPSY (MINOR) I, II 7, V 7, I (EX.289)
    MODAL
    ETC. ETC ,

ANALYZE THE FOLLOWING ROOT PROGRESSIONS AND WRITE OR FAKE ON PIANO MELODIES OVER EACH ONE:

MAKE UP SOME PROGRESSIONS, ALWAYS WORKING BACK FROM END OF PHRASE AND WRITE SIMPLE MELODIES OVER THEM

ANALYZE ROOT PROGRESSIONS IN SEVERAL POP TUNES

STUDY THE FORM OF SEVERAL POP TUNES.
   NOTICE THAT MOST HAVE AN **AABA** OR **ABAC** FORM.

A 8 BARS	A 8 BARS
A 8 BARS	B 8 BARS
B 8 BARS	A 8 BARS
A 8 BARS (OR 10 BARS)	C 8 BARS

FIND AN EXAMPLE OR TWO OF EACH OF THESE FORMS

   IN THE FIRST FORM THE THEME "A" STATES ITSELF AND IS REPEATED EXCEPT IT USUALLY ENDS MORE FINALLY THE SECOND TIME. THIS COMPLETES OUR FIRST SECTION OF 16 BARS (A A).

   THE SECOND THEME (OFTEN CALLED BRIDGE, OR RELEASE, OR CONTRASTING THEME) ALMOST INVARIABLY STARTS IN A NEW KEY. ONCE THE SECOND THEME IS ON ITS WAY, IT SEEMS ITS PURPOSE IS TO WORK BACK TO THE DOMINANT OF OUR ORIGINAL KEY. (B)

   OUR THIRD SECTION IS A RETURN TO OUR FIRST THEME WHICH FINISHES THE SONG. (A)

   ABA OR THE THREE PART FORM IS THE BASIC FORM OF ALL ART(OR ALL LIFE) FORM IS JUST RHYTHM ON A LARGER SCALE.
IN SOME OF THE LARGER SYMPHONIC FORMS THEY CALL ABA THE STATEMENT (OR MAIN THEME), SUBORDINATE THEME (OR CONTRASTING THEME), AND RECAPITULATION.
   YOU WILL FIND THIS THREE PART FORM IN SMALL COMPOSITIONS, POP TUNES, SYMPHONY MOVEMENTS, ARCHITECTURE, PAINTING, POETRY, RELIGION, BIOLOGY, ETC., ETC , ETC .

   WHEN WRITING A POP TUNE YOU MAY START WITH A CHORD (ROOT) PROGRESSION, BUT IT IS ALWAYS PREFERABLE TO START WITH A THEME OR A FRAGMENT OF A THEME. MANY TUNES HAVE BEEN WRITTEN FROM JUST A TITLE. SOME WRITERS TENTATIVELY SET A LYRIC (WORDS) FOR THE FIRST 8 BARS, AND THEN WRITE THE COMPLETE TUNE BEFORE FINISHING THE LYRIC. THEY SHOULD BE WORKED OUT TOGETHER AND BE MATED PERFECTLY IN MOOD, STYLE, RHYTHM, ETC.,

   BE SURE YOUR TUNE (EVEN IF IT IS A BALLAD) IS RHYTHMICALLY SIMPLE AND SOUND.
   RHYTHM, BEING THE MOST BASIC ELEMENT IN MUSIC SHOULD GET 1ST CONSIDERATION.
   MELODY IS NEXT IN IMPORTANCE.
   HARMONY COMES THIRD.

TRY A SIMPLE BASIC RHYTHM AND WRITE A SIMPLE MELODY TO IT.

THE RHYTHM OF YOUR MELODY MUST BE SIMPLE BUT STILL HAVE ENOUGH VARIETY TO KEEP FROM BEING MONOTONOUS.

ANALYZE SEVERAL POP TUNES RHYTHMICALLY.

ALTERED CHORDS

WE CAN ALTER A NOTE IN ANY CHORD BY BENDING THE NOTE TOWARD ITS RESOLUTION. IE: THE SECOND VOICE IN EX. 290 MOVES FROM A TO G WHICH IS A WHOLE STEP. WE CAN ALTER THE A TO A♭ SO IT WILL RESOLVE BY A HALF STEP, WHICH RESULTS IN AN ALTERED CHORD (D MIN 7TH - FLAT FIFTH)

290.

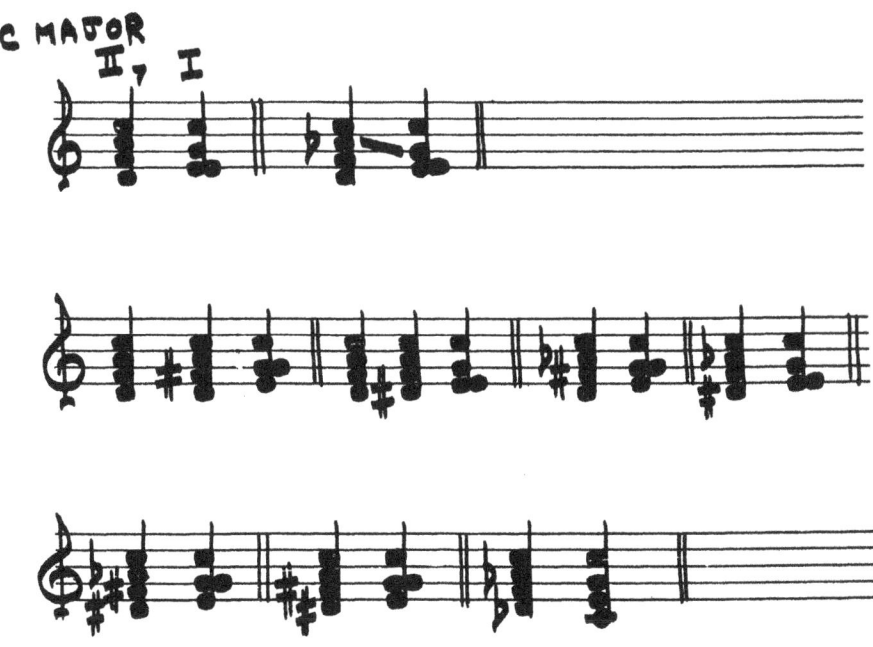

290. (CONTINUED)

THE SUBSTITUTE DOMINANT (CHORD BUILT ON THE FLAT FIFTH OF THE DOMINANT CHORD) CAN BE CONSIDERED AN ALTERED CHORD ALSO. (SEE EX.290)

IN PLACE OF THE COMMON C F C SO OFTEN FOUND IN THE FIFTEENTH AND SIXTEENTH BAR, OR ON THE ENDING OF A POP TUNE WE CAN USE

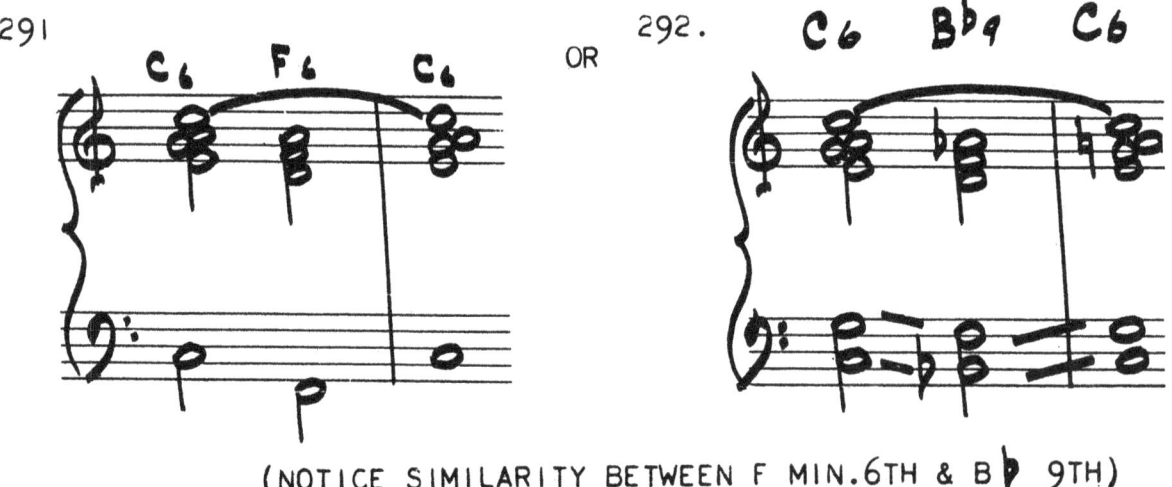

(NOTICE SIMILARITY BETWEEN F MIN.6TH & B♭ 9TH)

PARALLEL FIFTHS ARE ONLY FORBIDDEN IN TRIADS (THREE NOTE CHORDS)
ANY DISSONANCE (EVEN MILD DISSONANCE) MAKES PARALLEL FIFTHS SOUND
PLEASANT, COLORFUL, AND DESIREABLE.

ALSO INSTEAD OF C F C TRY:

  C, A FLAT NINTH, C.
  C, F NINTH, C.
  C, D FLAT MAJ.7TH, C.
  C, E FLAT, G FLAT, A, C,
  C, D FLAT, E FLAT, D FLAT, C.
  C, B FLAT 7TH, A FLAT 7TH, B FLAT 7TH, C.

USE SUBSTITUTE CHORDS SPARINGLY!!!

WHEN SUBSTITUTING A CHORD FOR ANY GIVEN CHORD IN A POP TUNE, USE
AN EXTREMELY DISTANT CHORD. IE: AN F CHORD SUBSTITUTED FOR A C CHORD
WILL SOUND LIKE A MISTAKE. IT IS ALWAYS MORE SATISFACTORY IF YOUR
MELODY NOTE BECOMES A MORE INTERESTING NOTE OF THE CHORD, IE: AUG.11TH,
OR A 13TH, OR A 3RD, OR A RAISED 9TH, ETC.)
WHEN SUBSTITUTING ALWAYS USE A MORE COLORFUL CHORD THAN THE ORIGINAL.
USE A CHORD WITH MORE TENSION,
    OR A CHORD WITH A DOMINANT 7TH FEELING, (ANY CHORD CONTAINING A
    TRITONE (AUG.4TH, DIM.5TH) HAS A DOMINANT 7TH FEELING)

TO FIND ALL THE SUBSTITUTE CHORDS FOR ANY MELODY NOTE THINK OF IT
FIRST AS A ROOT, THEN A 3RD, THEN A 5TH, 7TH, 9TH, 11TH, 13TH --
THEN CHECK THE SUSPENSIONS THAT ARE OF PRACTICAL USE.
  IE:
293.

COULD BE ROOT OF A MAJ, A 7TH, 9TH, 11TH, 13TH
OR ROOT OF A MIN, A MIN.6TH, A MIN.7TH
OR ROOT OF A DIM, A AUG, ETC., ETC.

COULD BE THE 3RD OF F MAJ, F 7TH, 9TH, 11TH, 13TH
OR THE 3RD OF F# MIN.6TH, 7TH, ETC.

COULD BE THE 5TH OF D MAJ, D 7TH, 9TH, ETC, ETC.

294.

WHEN LOOKING FOR SUBSTITUTE CHORDS ALWAYS WORK BACKWARDS FROM ANY STRONG POINT. IN EX. 294 LOOK BACK FROM THE C CHORD IN BAR 7. A STRONG ROOT PROGRESSION WOULD BE UP A 4TH, OR DOWN A HALF STEP, OR UP A WHOLE STEP.
   (G TO C, D♭ TO C, OR B♭ TO C) SEE EX. 269.
SO BAR 6 COULD BE SOME FORM OF G 7TH, (WITH ANY ADDITION OR ALTERATION) OR SOME FORM OF A D♭ 7TH, (11+), OR B♭ 9TH, (13TH)

LOOK FOR SUBSTITUTE CHORDS FOR BAR 2 BY LOOKING BACK FROM BAR 3. LOOK FOR STRONG ROOT PROGRESSIONS. (E 7TH 9+ WOULD BE ONE, B♭ 9TH, OR G MIN.6TH, OR E MIN.7TH (5-) WOULD ALSO BE GOOD POSSIBILITIES)

LOOKING FOR PARALLELS IS ANOTHER WAY OF LOOKING FOR SUBSTITUTE CHORDS. IN EX.295 WE MAY GO FROM THE C CHORD IN BAR 1 TO THE A 9TH CHORD IN BAR 3 THROUGH A B♭ 9TH (13TH)

295.

ANOTHER COMMON PRACTICE IS TO DELAY THE DOM.7TH CHORD BY USING A II 7 CHORD AHEAD OF IT. (D MIN.7TH TO G 7TH)

SOMETIMES SUBSTITUTE CHORDS ARE DERIVED AS A RESULT OF CONTRAPUNTAL LINES (SEE EX.318) BUT A LITTLE SKILL IN COUNTERPOINT IS REQUIRED TO USE THIS METHOD SUCCESSFULLY.

TAKE SEVERAL POP TUNES AND FIND SEVERAL SUBSTITUTE CHORDS IN EACH USING THE FIRST THREE METHODS GIVEN :
   1) ALTERING GIVEN CHORDS (EX.291, 290) & (EX. 97 TO 102)
   2) WORKING BACK FROM ANY STRONG RHYTHMIC OR HARMONIC POINT AND FINDING STRONG ROOT PROGRESSIONS. (EX.296)
   3) LOOKING FOR PARALLELS TO BRIDGE AN INTERVAL BETWEEN TWO STRONG POINTS (EX.295)

USE SUBSTITUTE CHORDS SPARINGLY!!!

296.
WORKING BACK FROM THE C ROOT THROUGH STRONG ROOT PROGRESSIONS, WE CAN FIND THE POSSIBLE GOOD PROGRESSIONS.

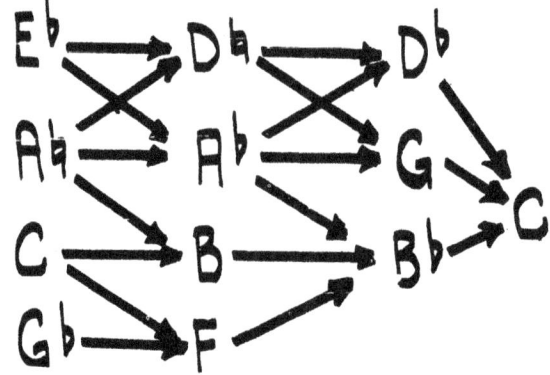

129

(A FEW POSSIBLE SUBSTITUTE CHORDS)
297.

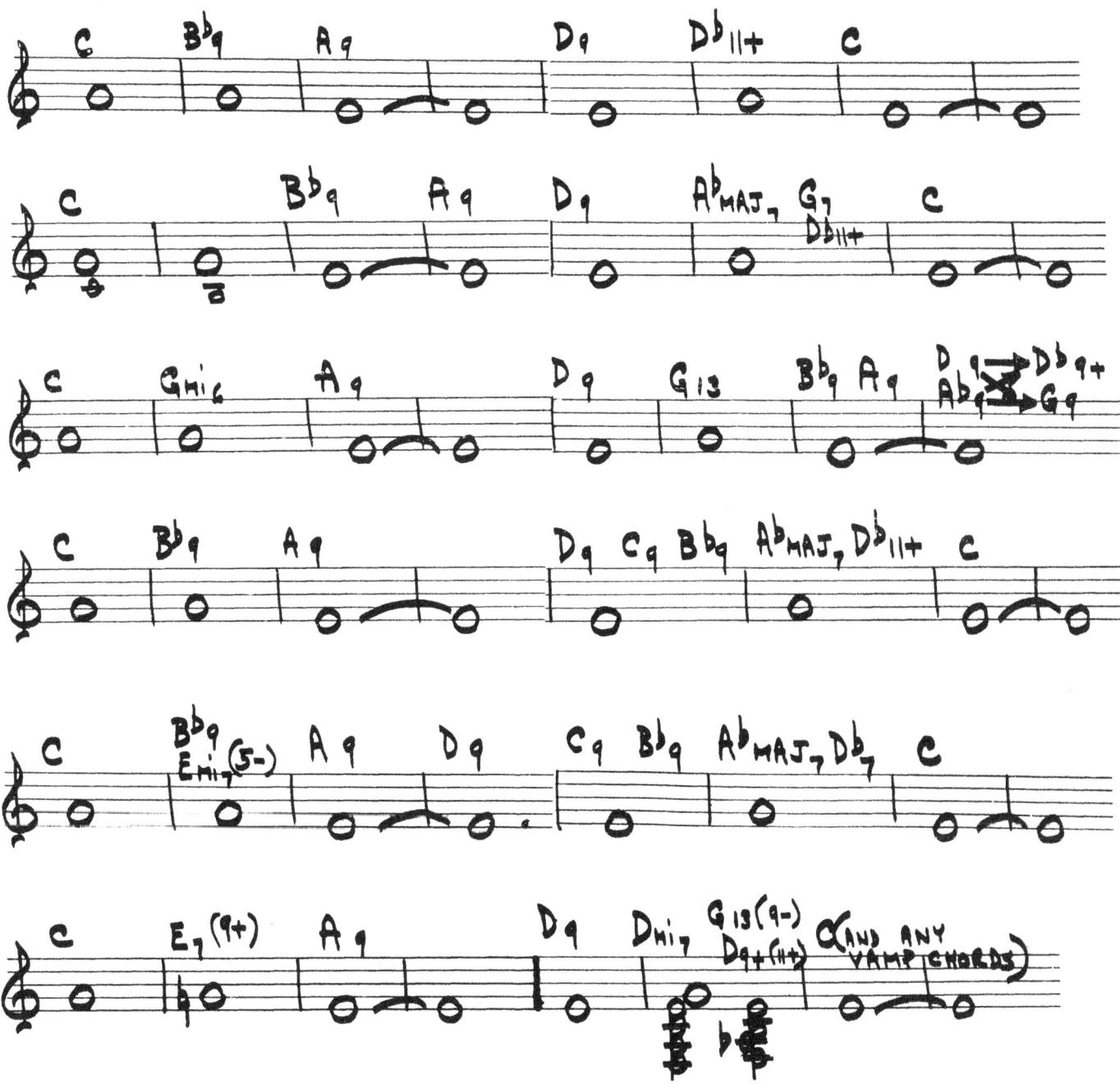

MELODY WRITING

IN TRADITIONAL HARMONY THEY USED TO TEACH US THAT THE 4TH STEP OF THE SCALE SHOULD MOVE DOWN AND THE 7TH STEP SHOULD MOVE UP, BUT THIS ONLY SEEMS TO APPLY TO DOMINANT 7TH TO TONIC HARMONIES.

WITH PRESENT DAY HARMONIES, A BETTER WAY OF PRESENTING THIS IDEA IS TO SAY THAT:
   THE INTERVAL OF A SEVENTH (MAJOR OR MINOR) WANTS TO BECOME SMALLER AND THE INTERVAL OF A SECOND WANTS TO BECOME LARGER.

298.

SO HARMONIES CAN AFFECT NOTE TENDENCIES. IN EX.299, THE E (3RD STEP OF THE C SCALE) IS STATIC IN THE C MAJ. CHORD, BUT IN THE G 7TH CHORD IT IS DYNAMIC BECAUSE OF THE MAJ.7TH INTERVAL BETWEEN IT AND THE F BELOW IT.

299.

A LARGE SKIP (INTERVAL) WANTS TO TURN BACK BY SMALLER INTERVALS.

300.   OR   301.

AND VICE VERSA, A SCALE PASSAGE WANTS TO TURN BACK BY A LARGER INTERVAL.

302.

IN A MELODIC PHRASE THE CLIMAX (HIGHEST NOTE) SHOULD ONLY OCCUR ONCE. (SOME SCHOOLS TEACH THAT THE LOWEST NOTE IN THE PHRASE SHOULD LIKEWISE ONLY OCCUR ONCE.)

THE REPETITION OF A PORTION OF THE PHRASE (FRAGMENT) CONTAINING THE CLIMACTIC NOTE IS ONE EXCEPTION.

PREFERABLY THE CLIMACTIC NOTE IS NEAR THE END OF THE PHRASE.

303.

A CLIMAX TOWARD THE END OF THE CHORUS, THAT TOPS THE CLIMAX OF THE PHRASES BEFORE IT, IS VERY NICE ALSO.

A CLIMAX TOWARD THE END OF AN ARRANGEMENT OR COMPOSITION, THAT TOPS EVERYTHING THAT HAS GONE BEFORE IT, IS ALSO VERY EFFECTIVE.

304.

A MELODIC SKIP CREATES A TENSION AND CREATES A DESIRE TO HEAR THE SCALE NOTES IN BETWEEN. IN EX. 304, THE SKIP C DOWN TO D CREATES A DESIRE IN OUR MIND TO HEAR THE NOTES IN THE F MAJOR SCALE THAT WE SKIPPED OVER. (B♭,A,G,F,E) A SUBTLE MELODY DOESN'T ANSWER THAT DESIRE IMMEDIATELY BUT KEEPS OUR INTEREST BY HOLDING US OFF (TEASING US A LITTLE BIT). IN LITERATURE, RADIO, TV, AND FILMS THIS IS CALLED THE UNANSWERED QUESTION OR THE NARRATIVE HOOK. IN MUSIC WE ACCOMPLISH THIS BY HARMONIC TENSION, AND MOTION, AS WELL AS BY THE UNFULLFILLED TENSION THAT MELODIC SKIPS CREATE.

NOTICE IN BAR 2 OF EX 304, WE HEAR E,F, AND A BUT G IS HELD OFF UNTIL BAR 4. IN BAR 3, WE HAVE ANOTHER SKIP BUT THE INTERVAL IS FILLED IN BARS 4 AND 5. JUST AS WE FEEL SECURE, THE MELODY SKIPS FROM E TO A, LEAVING A DESIRE TO HEAR F AND G. NOTICE THAT THE F IS HELD OFF UNTIL THE 2ND ENDING. HINDEMITH, IN HIS BOOK, "CRAFT OF MUSICAL COMPOSITION" ALSO SPEAKS OF SUBTLE SCALE PROGRESSIONS WITHIN A MELODY. IN EX 304, THE C IN BAR 1, THE D IN BAR 3, AND THE E IN BAR 5 FORM A SCALE PASSAGE. LOOK FOR OTHER SCALE PROGRESSIONS IN EX 304.

DON'T WRITE MELODIES BY RULES!!!
WRITE A MELODY AND THEN SEE IF IT HOLDS UP TO THE RULES.
    DOES YOUR MELODY HAVE SIMPLE AND LOGICAL RHYTHM? (TAP RHYTHM OF MELODY IN EX.261)
    DOES HARMONY CHANGE AT THE RIGHT PLACES RHYTHMICALLY?
    DO LARGE SKIPS TURN BACK WITH SMALLER INTERVALS?
    DO SCALE PASSAGES TURN BACK BY SKIPS?
    DOES CLIMAX NOTE OCCUR JUST ONCE? (SEE EXCEPTIONS PAGE 116)
    ARE ALL SKIP TENSIONS RELIEVED?
    IS THE HARMONIC PROGRESSION GOOD? (SEE EX.269)
    IS THE METER OF THE PHRASES NATURAL? (FORM)

ANALYZE EX.304 AND SEVERAL OTHER COMPOSITIONS OR SONGS.
WRITE SOME ORIGINAL SONGS AND THEN ANALYZE THEM IN THE ABOVE MANNER.

    SEE HOW MANY FAULTS YOU CAN FIND WITH THE FOLLOWING MELODY.
                  (THERE ARE PLENTY!)

305.

TO ADVANCE FURTHER ANY ARRANGER SHOULD STUDY:

1) HARMONY AND COUNTERPOINT
    FROM A TEACHER WHO IS WORKING AS AN ACTIVE AND COMPETENT COMPOSER AND ARRANGER. A MUSICOLOGIST OR A TEACHER WHO CAN'T COMPOSE AND ARRANGE WILL OFTEN LOAD YOU WITH UNNECESSARY MATERIAL AND MAKE THE ROAD TEDIOUS AND BORING, AND THREE TIMES LONGER. I DON'T MEAN BY THIS THAT YOU CAN LEARN IT IN "TEN EASY LESSONS"; IT'S GOING TO TAKE AT LEAST TWO YEARS OF CONCENTRATED STUDY AND THEN YOU WILL BE STUDYING AND ANALYZING ON YOUR OWN FOR THE REST OF YOUR LIFE.

2) FORM
   COMPOSITION
   ORCHESTRATION
    BY COMPOSING (UNDER GUIDANCE) FOR CHAMBER GROUPS, OR SOLO INSTRUMENTS, OR ORCHESTRA IN THE DIFFERENT FORMS
    (3 PART SONG FORM, RONDO FORMS, SONATA ALLEGRO FORMS, THE CONTRAPUNTAL FORMS, AND THE VARIATION FORMS)

3) SOLFEGE
    WHICH INCLUDES THE ART OF RELATING SOUNDS WITH THE SYMBOLS WE USE TO REPRESENT THEM ON PAPER. (MELODIC DICTATION, CHORD RECOGNITION, AND CHORD PROGRESSION RECOGNITION, SIGHT SINGING, TONAL MEMORY, TRANSPOSING A PHRASE AT A TIME BY SYLLABLES, COPYING RECORDS, INTERVAL PRACTICE, RECOGNIZING WHAT NOTE OF THE CHORD IS IN THE MELODY, ETC.)

4) LEARN AS MUCH ABOUT EVERY INSTRUMENT AS YOU CAN. LEARN TO PLAY A LITTLE ON EACH ONE.

5) STUDY AND PRACTICE CONDUCTING.

6) LEARN TO COMPOSE ALL TYPES OF MUSIC.
    INCLUDING FREE (ATONAL) COUNTERPOINT, AND THE "12 TONE TECHNIQUE"

7) LISTEN ANALYTICALLY AND STUDY SCORES AND RECORDS.

8) READ ALL THE BOOKS YOU CAN ON THE SUBJECT OF WRITING MUSIC.
    STUDY: FORSYTHE - "ORCHESTRATION"
            HINDEMITH - "CRAFT OF MUSICAL COMPOSITION"
            TOCH - "SHAPING FORCES IN MUSIC"

9) WRITE AND WRITE AND WRITE SOME MORE!!!
    TRY TO HAVE EVERYTHING YOU WRITE PLAYED SO THAT YOU CAN HEAR IT AND LEARN FROM IT.

FREEDOM OF EXPRESSION

WHEN YOU ARE WRITING MUSIC

1) FEEL FREE!! LET IDEAS COME TO YOU.
   TAKE OFF ANY TIGHT JEWELERY, WATCHES, NECKTIES, ETC.

2) BE ALONE IF POSSIBLE.

3) DON'T THINK IN NOTES. HEAR THE INSTRUMENTS PLAYING IN YOUR IMAGINATION. THEN TRANSLATE THESE SOUNDS INTO NOTES AS NEARLY AS YOU POSSIBLY CAN. LEARN TO THINK OR CREATE ON THE UNSPEAKABLE LEVEL.

4) SING OUT LOUD!!
   IF YOU GET STUCK, GO BACK TO THE PHRASE BEFORE AND SING OUT LOUD AND WHEN YOU COME TO THE SPOT YOU WERE STUCK YOU CAN'T HELP BUT SING RIGHT ON. THEN ALL YOU HAVE TO DO IS WRITE DOWN WHAT YOU SANG.

5) AFTER YOU HAVE HAD A LITTLE EXPERIENCE, YOU WILL FIND THAT YOUR FIRST IDEAS ARE USUALLY THE BEST.

6) IF YOU CAN LEARN TO BELIEVE THAT MUSIC ALL COMES FROM SOME MAIN SOURCE OUTSIDE OF YOURSELF OR WITHIN YOURSELF, AND BELIEVE THAT YOUR JOB IS TO PUT IT DOWN ON PAPER IN IT'S BEST POSSIBLE FORM, IT WILL HELP YOU A LOT. THIS HAS FREED MANY STUDENTS OF MENTAL BLOCKS THAT WOULDN'T LET THEM EXPRESS THEMSELVES FREELY.
   (THIS WAY IF IT TURNS OUT BAD IT'S NOT YOUR FAULT)

7) LEARN TO WRITE RHYTHMIC CURVES.
   THINK FIRST RHYTHMICALLY, THEN THE GENERAL MELODIC CURVE OF THE MELODY OR COUNTER MELODY. THEN THE ACTUAL NOTES AND HARMONIES ARE SIMPLE TO PUT IN.

   WITH THIS SYSTEM YOU CAN BLOCK OUT THE WHOLE ARRANGEMENT MUCH FASTER AND KEEP THE PICTURE OF THE WHOLE, WHICH MAKES FOR BETTER CONTINUITY AND CONSISTANCY. SO MANY ARRANGERS GET SO WRAPPED UP IN EACH LITTLE VOICING OR HARMONY, THEY LOSE THE FLOW, AND TEMPO, AND THE PICTURE OF THE ARRANGEMENT AS A WHOLE.
   (A PAINTER SKETCHES THE GENERAL OUTLINE OF HIS PICTURE BEFORE HE GOES BACK AND PUTS IN ALL OF THE DETAILS)

SOME HINTS ON CONDUCTING

IT IS ALWAYS MORE SATISFACTORY IF AN ARRANGER CAN REHEARSE HIS ARRANGEMENTS. SOME SMALL CONDUCTORS IN BIG JOBS DON'T LIKE YOU TO, BUT THE MAJORITY OF COMPETENT CONDUCTORS WILL APPRECIATE THE HELP YOU CAN GIVE THEM IN MAKING THE ORCHESTRA AND THE ARRANGEMENT SOUND GOOD.

LEARN THE BASIC BEATS (4/4, 3/4, 2/4, ¢, 5/4, 6/4, 7/4, ETC., 6/8, 9/8, 12/8, ETC.) AND ALL OF THESE SUBDIVIDED (WITH EITHER OR BOTH HANDS) AND THEN FORGET THEM. SING THE MUSIC INSIDE OF YOU AND LET YOUR HANDS FOLLOW NATURALLY.

THE CONDUCTORS MAIN FUNCTION IS TO REHEARSE THE ORCHESTRA WELL AND TO KEEP DISCIPLINE. (HE WILL HAVE DISCIPLINE IF THEY RESPECT HIS ABILITY. IF THEY DON'T RESPECT, THEN DEMANDING THEIR RESPECT IS A LAST RESORT.)

THE CONDUCTOR GETS ALL THE CREDIT BECAUSE THE PUBLIC CAN ACTUALLY SEE HIM DOING SOMETHING, WHILE THE COMPOSER ARRANGER IS JUST SOME MYSTERIOUS NECESSITY IN THE BACKGROUND.

90% OF THE TIME AN ORCHESTRA CAN PLAY THE PERFORMANCE BETTER WITHOUT A CONDUCTOR. (IN A DANCE BAND I MIGHT UP THAT TO 99%) BUT LEARN TO CONDUCT. IT INCREASES YOUR OPPORTUNITIES BY 3 OR 4 TIMES, AND WHO KNOWS BETTER HOW AN ARRANGEMENT OR A COMPOSITION SHOULD SOUND THAN THE MAN WHO WROTE IT.

EXPERIMENTAL MATERIAL FOR THE PROGRESSIVE ARRANGER COMPOSER

BOOK VI

PROGRESSIVE IDEAS FOR THE ADVANCED ARRANGER TO EXPERIMENT WITH.

1) PARALLEL HARMONIES
    TAKE ANY INTERVAL (2NDS, OR 5THS, OR 4THS, ETC.)
    AND LET IT MOVE PARALLEL. THEN WRITE A MELODY
    AGAINST IT. TRY TO HAVE THE MELODY MOVE UP IN
    CONTRAST TO A BACKGROUND THAT MOVES DOWN AND
    VICE VERSA. (OPPOSITE MOTION)

306.

PARALLEL 4THS

WRITE A MELODY OVER THE FOLLOWING PARALLEL CHORDS. (EX.307)
NOTICE THAT PARALLEL DOES NOT NECESSARILY MEAN CHROMATIC.
PARALLELS MAY MOVE BY HALF STEPS, OR WHOLE STEPS, OR 3RDS, ETC,
OR ANY COMBINATION OF THEM, AND NEED NOT BE ALL IN ONE DIRECTION.

307.

WRITE A MELODIC PHRASE USING MINOR CHORDS.
CHOOSE ROOT PROMISCUOUSLY.
    IE:
308.

WRITE A MELODY FOR FLUTE OVER THE FOLLOWING CHORDS AND WRITE THE ACCOMPANIMENT FOR STRING QUARTET.

309.
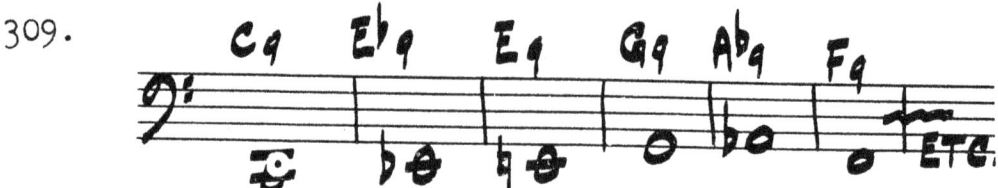

SOMETIMES WITH CHORD STRUCTURES THAT ARE ALL THE SAME TYPE, WE CAN USE VOICE LEADING INSTEAD OF MOVING ALL VOICES PARALLEL (EX.310-11)

THE EXAMPLES DO NOT MEAN MUCH BY THEMSELVES, BUT MAY BE THE BASIS FOR AN ACCOMPANIMENT, AND A MELODY MAY BE WRITTEN OVER THEM.

310.   311.
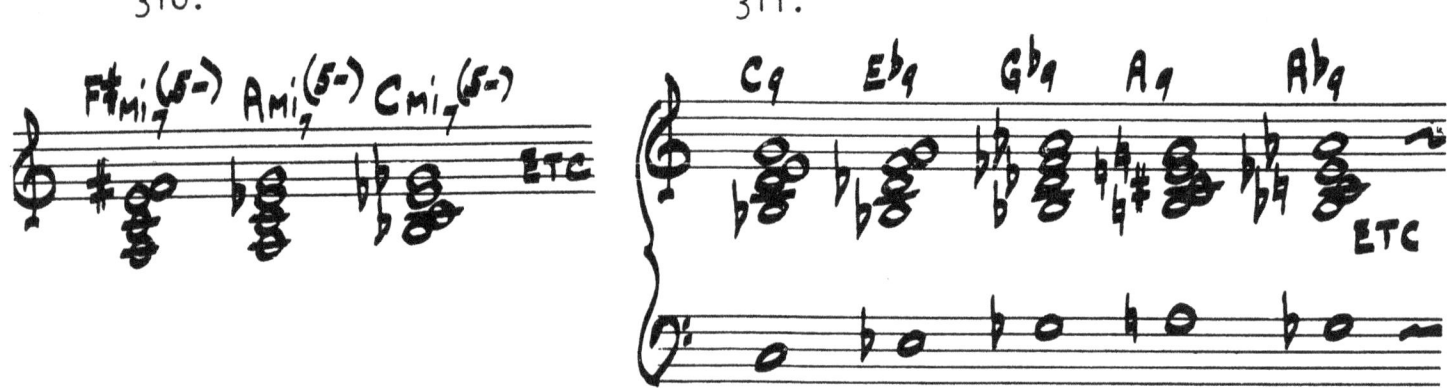

2) POLY-TONALITY
   WRITING IN TWO DIFFERENT KEYS SIMILTANEOUSLY. (EX.312) TO BE USED WITH DISCRETION! (SOME MODERN LEGITIMATE COMPOSERS HAVE UNSUCCESSFULLY BASED THEIR WHOLE STYLE ON THIS DEVICE)

312.

3) REFLECTIONS
   IN EX. 313 THE C MAJOR CHORD IS THE CENTER (MIRROR) AND
   THE D♮ CHORD IS CONSIDERED THE REFLECTION OF THE B MAJOR
   CHORD. THE D CHORD IS CONSIDERED THE REFLECTION OF THE
   B♭ CHORD, ETC. THIS CAN BE DONE WITH ANY NOTE, OR ANY
   TYPE OF CHORD, ALTHOUGH THE MAJOR CHORD SEEMS TO WORK
   OUT MOST SATISFACTORILY. SOME WRITERS HAVE USED THIS
   DEVICE TO WRITE POLYTONALITY. IE: D♭ MAJOR AGAINST
   B MAJOR, OR B♭ AGAINST D MAJOR, ETC.

313.

314.

REFLECTIONS OF CHORDS, CHOOSING THE ROOT OF A CHORD AS A CENTER.
(EX.315) NOTICE THE REFLECTION OF A MAJOR CHORD IS A MINOR CHORD
AND VICE VERSA - WRITE THE REFLECTIONS OF ALL THE OTHER CHORDS
(7THS, MIN.7THS, 9THS, ETC.)

315.

4) BUILDING CHORDS OUT OF OTHER INTERVALS THAN 3RDS
   (4THS, 5THS, 2NDS, ETC.)

316.

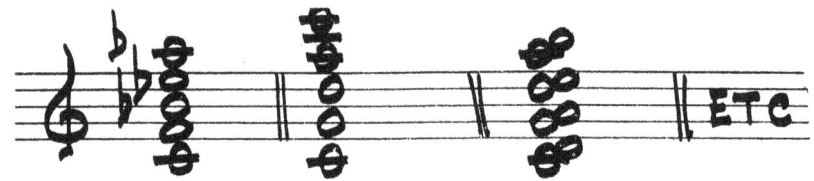

5) THE USE OF FREE CLUSTERS INSTEAD OF THE ORDINARY CHORDS WITHIN A KEY.
   WE MUST CONSIDER TENSION AND CONSISTENCY IN THIS STYLE OF WRITING. IE: DO NOT FOLLOW AN EXTREMELY DISSONANT CHORD (HIGH TENSION) WITH A SIMPLE TRIAD UNLESS YOU WANT IT TO SOUND COMIC. WE CAN ALSO FIND THE ROOTS OF CLUSTERS (SEE EX.263-7) TOWARD THE END OF A PHRASE OR SECTION IT IS NECESSARY TO HAVE A STRONG ROOT PROGRESSION. (EX.263-269)

317.

6) LINEAR HARMONY
   IN WHICH CHORDS ARE THE RESULT OF LINEAR (CONTRAPUNTAL) WRITING.
   IN EX. 318, THE SECOND CHORD IS A RESULT OF WRITING EACH INDIVIDUAL LINE FROM ONE ACCENTED BEAT TO ANOTHER. THE ADVANCED COUNTERPOINT STUDENT CAN WRITE FROM AN ACCENTED BEAT TO ANOTHER ACCENTED BEAT TWO OR FOUR MORE MEASURES AWAY AND ALL THE CHORDS IN BETWEEN WILL BE THE RESULT OF THE INDIVIDUAL LINES.

318.

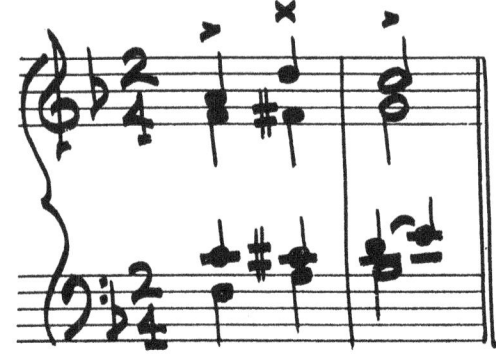

319.

EXAMPLES 318 TO 321 ARE ALL BUILT FROM THE SAME IDEA.
SOME USES OF COUNTERPOINT ARE TOUCHED UPON IN EX. 149 TO 158.

7) RHYTHMIC CURVES

THIS WONDERFUL WAY OF WRITING IS AN ART IN ITSELF. IF YOU CAN TRAIN YOUR MIND TO THINK IN THIS WAY IT IS AN INVALUABLE HELP IN COMPOSING AND ARRANGING BOTH DANCE AND LEGITIMATE MUSIC. YOU MUST THINK FIRST RHYTHMICALLY THEN MELODICALLY. IT IS WISE AT FIRST TO JUST WRITE GENERAL RHYTHMIC CURVES, NOT ACTUAL NOTES WITH TONALITIES. (EX. 322)

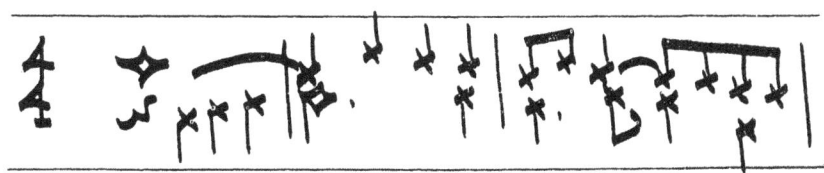

THIS WAY OF THINKING CAN BE APPLIED TO BRASS AGAINST SAXES OR VIOLINS AGAINST FRENCH HORN, ETC.

TAKE SEVERAL BALLADS AND WRITE A RHYTHMIC CURVE AGAINST THE MELODY THAT CONTRASTS RHYTHMICALLY WITH THE MELODY, AND ALSO USES OPPOSITE MOTION. ONCE YOU HAVE A GENERAL RHYTHMIC CURVE IT IS EASY TO FIND NOTES AND HARMONIES THAT ARE NATURAL TO IT. (EX. 322)
TRY THIS ALSO WITH A TUNE THAT HAS A BEAT TO IT.

USE ANY POP BALLAD & ANY POP SWING TUNE.

WHEN WRITING ATONAL MUSIC WITH THIS SYSTEM (WHICH IS MY FAVORITE WAY OF WRITING ATONAL MUSIC) BE SURE AND BUILD YOUR HARMONIES OUT OF THE INTERVALS THAT YOUR MELODY ASKS FOR. IE: THE MELODY IN EX. 349 IS MADE OF 4THS, MIN. 7THS, AND 5THS, SO THE HARMONIES THAT WILL SOUND THE MOST LOGICAL ARE CLUSTERS BUILT OUT OF THESE INTERVALS (AND THEIR INVERSIONS;) (THE INVERSION OF A MIN. 7TH IS A MAJ. 2ND, ETC.)

WRITING RHYTHMIC CURVES WILL SPEED YOUR COMPOSING AND ARRANGING AND HELP YOU KEEP THE PICTURE OF THE WHOLE COMPOSITION OR ARRANGEMENT IN YOUR MIND WHICH IS ALL IMPORTANT. IT IS SIMILAR TO AN ARTIST SKETCHING HIS PICTURE BEFORE GOING BACK TO PUT IN ALL THE DETAILS. OR AS AN AUTHOR OUTLINING THE PLOT OF HIS STORY BEFORE HE WRITES IT IN DETAIL.

RHYTHMIC CURVES
323.

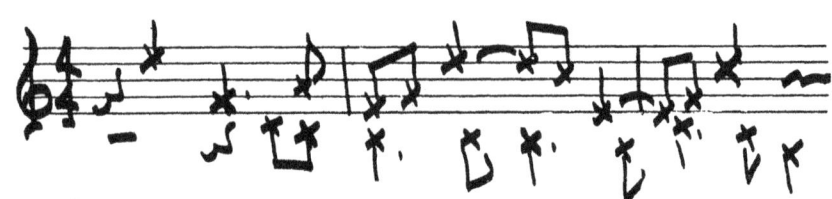

PUT INTO NOTES
324.

325.

8) WRITING MASS MOTION

THIS IS WRITING RHYTHMIC CURVES WITH MASSES OF SOUND. CONTRAST IN THE DIRECTION OF EACH MASS IS ESSENTIAL. THIS SYSTEM OF WRITING IS OFTEN REFERRED TO AS "PAINTING A SCORE." A CURVED OR JAGGED LINE ON THE SCORE PAGE IN ONE COLOR AND A COUNTER LINE OR TWO AGAINST IT IN A CONTRASTING OR SIMILAR COLOR. GOOD CLEAN TRANSPARENT ORCHESTRATION ALWAYS LOOKS NICE ON THE SCORE PAGE (LINES AND CONTRASTING LINES) WHETHER IT IS CONCEIVED IN THIS MASS MOTION MANNER OR NOT. (SEE EX. 326 TO 328)

MASS MOTION WRITING IS A WONDERFUL DEVICE, BUT DON'T EVER CONCEIVE MUSIC BY RULES OR MATHEMATICAL DEVICES. MUSIC MUST BE CONCEIVED ON THE UNSPEAKABLE LEVEL (AS INSPIRATION OR INTUITION) DON'T THINK IN NOTES, OR DON'T THINK FIRST IN TERMS OF CHARTS OR MUSIC STAVES.

LET YOUR THEMES BE GIFTS OF INSPIRATION AND THEN USE ALL YOUR KNOWLEDGE AND TECHNIQUE TO PUT THEM DOWN IN THE BEST POSSIBLE FORM.

SOME SYSTEMS RECOMMEND WRITING ON CHARTS. IN EX. 329 TIME VALUES CAN BE EIGHTH NOTES OR SIXTEENTH NOTES OR WHAT EVER DENOMINATOR YOU NEED; THE MOTION IS FROM THE LEFT. VERTICALLY ON THE CHART IS THE RISE AND FALL OF THE PITCH. FROM LEFT TO RIGHT IS THE RHYTHM AND UP AND DOWN ARE THE NOTES OF OUR SCALE. SOME COMPOSERS THAT USE THIS SYSTEM WRITE THE DIFFERENT COLORS OF THE ORCHESTRA IN DIFFERENT COLORED INK OR PENCIL.

329.   "WAY DOWN UPON THE SWANEE RIVER"

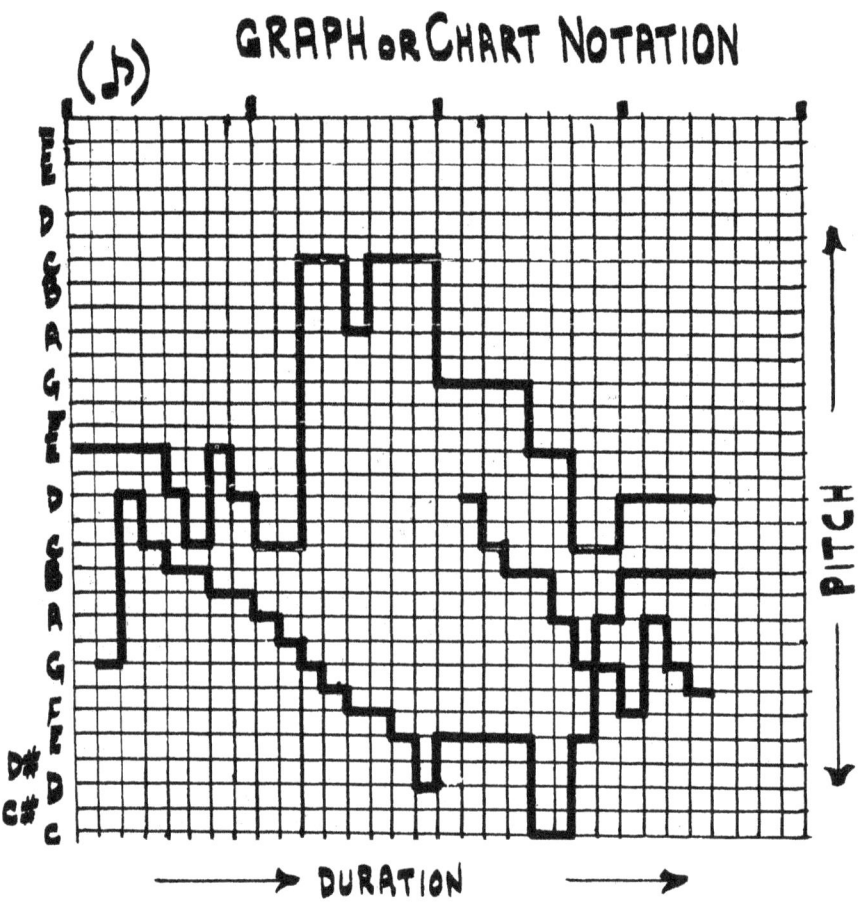

329-A.

TRANSLATE EX. 329 & 329-A INTO REGULAR MUSIC NOTATION.

9) SCALES MAY BE BUILT FROM CHORDS OR MELODIES.

THE INTERVAL C TO E♭ MAY BE BRIDGED IN THE FOLLOWING WAYS,

330.

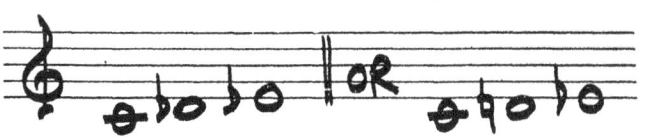

THE INTERVAL E♭ TO G MAY BE BRIDGED IN THE FOLLOWING WAYS,

331.

THE FOUR MOST LIKELY WAYS TO BRIDGE THE INTERVAL G TO C ARE,

332.

SO YOU CAN SEE THE C MINOR CHORD MAY INSPIRE MORE THAN TWENTY-FOUR DIFFERENT 7 NOTE SCALES.

THE CHORD IN EX. 333 MAY GIVE US SEVERAL SCALES BY BRINGING ALL THE NOTES OF THE CHORD INTO ONE OCTAVE, AND THEN BRIDGING THE GAPS IF NECESSARY.

333.

334.

THE MELODIC LINE IN EX. 335 WILL GIVE US THE FOLLOWING SCALES,

335.
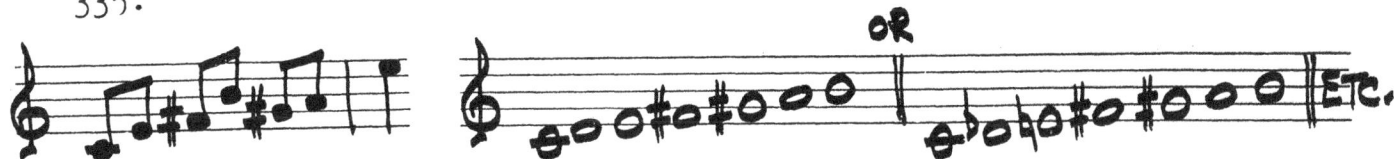

CONSIDERATION MUST BE GIVEN TO THE CHORD BEFORE AND THE CHORD FOLLOWING WHEN CHOOSING THE SCALE NOTES TO BRIDGE A GAP.

THE WHOLE TONE SCALE, AND THE MODAL SCALES, AND ALL THE MINOR SCALES ARE COVERED SO FULLY IN OTHER TEXTS, I DON'T THINK IT IS NECESSARY TO SAY ANYTHING ABOUT THEM HERE.

10) DOUBLING MELODY (OR ANY INTERESTING LINE) WITH PARALLEL INTERVALS. (4THS, 5THS, 2NDS, 7THS, ETC.) (SOMETIMES CALLED COUPLINGS)

336.

11) YOU MAY USE NON-CHORDAL TONES (SUSPENSIONS ABOVE OR BELOW) (OR PASSING NOTES) WITHOUT RESOLUTION.

337.   338.

12) ORGAN POINT.
   ONE NOTE (OR CHORD, OR SHORT MOTIVE) MAY PERSIST (THROUGH A SHORT PASSAGE) AGAINST MELODIES OR HARMONIES TO WHICH IT DOES NOT NORMALLY BELONG. EX. 339, THE C AND G IN BASS CLEF ARE AN ORGAN POINT.

339.

340.

WRITE AN INTRO TO SOME SONG USING ORGAN POINT.

13) WANDERING HARMONIES

IN EX.341, NOTICE THAT THE NOTES IN THE CHORD PROGRESSION. FEEL THEIR WAY BY HALF STEP OR WHOLE STEP (ONE OR TWO OR THREE VOICES AT A TIME) ROOT PROGRESSION IS IGNORED. THE PROGRESSION SOUNDS LOGICAL BECAUSE OF THE SMOOTH VOICE LEADING IN ALL THE PARTS. (341)
(RAVEL- DAPHNES AND CHLOE SUITE II,176 TO 179) CHOPIN, WAGNER, RICHARD STRAUSS ALL USED THIS DEVICE EFFECTIVELY.

341.

14) IMITATIONS

342.

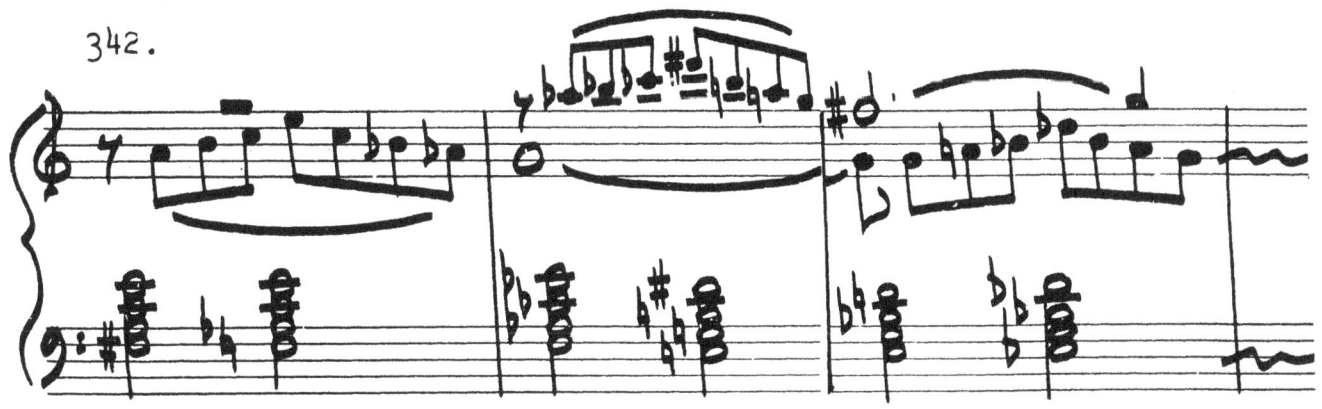

ALSO SEE EX.158 (IMITATIONS)

15) MELODIC SEQUENCES
ARE REPETITIONS STARTING ON A HIGHER OR LOWER PITCH THAN
THE ORIGINAL. NOTICE EX.343 STAYS WITHIN THE KEY, WHILE
EX.344 WHICH IS AN EXACT SEQUENCE WANDERS THROUGH SEVERAL
KEYS. ALSO NOTICE THAT WHILE SEQUENCES GIVE US UNITY IT
IS USUALLY CUSTOMARY TO VARY THE THIRD OR FOURTH SEQUENCE
FOR VARIETY. (THE SAME APPLIES TO RHYTHMIC AND HARMONIC
SEQUENCES)

343.

344.

DOUBLE, TRIPLE, SEQUENCES, ETC.
IN EX.345, THE MELODY WHICH STARTS ON THE 5TH OF THE 9TH
CHORD IS LED INTO ANOTHER NOTE OF A CHORD OF THE SAME TYPE
(THE 9TH OF A B 9TH CHORD.) THIS ENABLES ANOTHER VOICE
TO CARRY ON THE SEQUENCE, ETC.
THESE SOUND WONDERFUL IF EACH SEQUENCE MOVES INTO A NICE
FRESH CHORD CHANGE.

WRITE A DANCE BAND MODULATION USING THIS DEVICE. (USE A
FRAGMENT OF THE MELODY FOR YOUR SEQUENCE)

345.

SEQUENCES USUALLY BUILD EITHER UP OR DOWN AND CAN BE VERY
EXCITING

16) TRICK CANNONS

IN EX. 346 EACH LINE FITS AGAINST THE OTHER LINES SO IF WE MAKE A MELODY BY JUXTAPOSING THE FOUR LINES (EX. 347) WE CAN MAKE A FOUR VOICE CANNON (EX. 348) NOTICE THAT EACH VOICE IS IMITATING THE VOICE ABOVE IT, BUT ONE BAR LATER.

346.

347.

348.

17) MELODIES WILL OFTEN DENOTE THE TYPE OF HARMONIES THAT ARE REQUIRED IN EX.349 THE MELODY CONTAINS THE INTERVALS PERF.4TH, MIN.7TH, PERF.5TH, SO HARMONIES BUILT FROM INTERVALS OF THIS TYPE (AND THEIR INVERSIONS) WILL SOUND CONVINCING AGAINST THIS MELODY.

349.

18) OUT OF METER PHRASES MAY BE EFFECTIVE (WRITTEN PURPOSELY) IF THEY ARE JUSTIFIED BY REPETITION.

19) SCHOENBERG 12 TONE TECHNIQUE
THE USE OF THE SCHOENBERG TONE ROW TECHNIQUE CAN BE EFFECTIVE (IF USED WITH DISCRETION) FOR THOSE WHO WANT TO WRITE "ATONAL" MUSIC. IT IS GOOD TO BECOME PROFFICIENT IN THIS TECHNIQUE OF WRITING IF ONLY FOR THE PRACTICE IT GIVES YOU IN WRITING RHYTHMIC CURVES. "STUDIES IN COUNTERPOINT" BY ERNST KRENEK IS A GOOD BOOK TO LEARN THE BASIC FACTORS OF THIS TYPE OF WRITING.

IT IS HEALTHY TO LEARN ALL YOU CAN ABOUT EVERY TYPE OF MUSIC AND THEN LET YOUR OWN CONSCIENCE, INTUITION, AND REASONING PICK THE PARTS OF EACH THAT BEST HELP YOU TO EXPRESS YOUR IDEAS, EMOTIONS, AND INSPIRATIONS; NATURALLY, HONESTLY, AND SINCERELY.

20) IT IS INTERESTING TO NOTE THAT MANY OF THE EXTENSIONS OF OUR DOMINANT 7TH WILL FORM MAJOR TRIADS. (EX.350)

350.

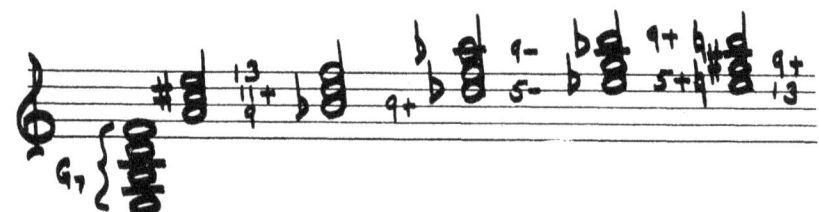

21) METHOD OF PROCEDURE FOR TRADITIONAL HARMONY EXERCISE (CHORALE) SEEMS OUT OF THE SCOPE OF THIS BOOK BUT SINCE IT IS SORELY NEEDED AND NOT PRINTED ELSEWHERE, THAT I KNOW OF, HERE IT IS:

351.

1) SING THE MELODY AND DECIDE ON POSSIBLE CHORD STRUCTURES FOR MAIN ACCENTS (USUALLY THE FIRST BEAT OF EACH BAR) IN EX.351 THE STYLE OF THE MELODY SEEMS TO ASK FOR SIMPLE CHORD STRUCTURES.
THE I, IV, II 7, AND V 7, OR V9 CHORDS IN E MINOR ARE:

352.

IN EX.351 THE FIRST BAR WANTS A I CHORD; THE SECOND BAR A II 7 OR V 7; THIRD BAR II 7 OR V 7; FOURTH BAR A I CHORD, ETC.

2) WRITE THE BOTTOM LINE (CELLO) KEEPING GOOD INTERVALS BETWEEN THE TOP AND BOTTOM VOICES (EX.353) THESE TWO LINES MOST ALWAYS HELP YOU DETERMINE WHICH CHORDS WILL BE MOST SATISFACTORY.

GOOD INTERVALS ARE 3RDS, 6THS, 2NDS, AND 7THS.
PERFECT 5THS AND OCTAVES MAY BE USED AT THE BEGINNING AND ENDING OF PHRASES, OR IN BETWEEN TWO GOOD INTERVALS (ANY PERFECT INTERVAL BETWEEN TOP AND BOTTOM VOICE GIVES US STRENGTH. OTHER INTERVALS GIVE US BEAUTY. WE NEED THE STRENGTH USUALLY FOR ENDS OF PHRASES OR SECTIONS.

WHEN WRITING ANY LINE WORRY ABOUT THE CHORDS ON THE ACCENTED BEATS, BUT IN BETWEEN ACCENTS JUST WRITE LINES THAT SOUND AGAINST WHAT YOU HAVE.

NOTICE IN EX. 353 THAT SOMETIMES CONTRARY MOTION IS USED AND AND SOMETIMES PARALLEL MOTION. TOO MUCH CONTRARY MOTION CAN BECOME MONOTONOUS.

3) WRITE SMOOTH INNER PARTS (VLN II, VIOLA). EACH VOICE SHOULD MAKE GOOD SENSE (RHYTHMICALLY AND MELODICALLY) BY ITSELF.
IN WRITING EACH VOICE WORK FROM ACCENT TO ACCENT ALWAYS WORKING TOWARD A GOAL (THE VOICING ON THE NEXT ACCENT)

I WOULD SUGGEST WORKING AWAY FROM THE PIANO. WRITE, THEN SING IT, AND THEN PLAY IT. NOTICE THE SUSPENSIONS ADDED IN BAR 2, BAR 4, ETC. TO BE CONSISTENT WITH THE STYLE OF THE MELODY IN BAR 3. ALSO NOTICE SOME OF THE CHORDS OFF OF THE ACCENTS THAT WERE THE RESULT OF LINES. ALSO THE RHYTHM IS COMPLETE. SOME VOICE IS MOVING ON EVERY QUARTER NOTE. A STRONG ROOT PROGRESSION IS USED AT THE END OF EACH PHRASE. ALSO NOTICE THAT THE TRITE MAJOR 3RD IS NOT USED IN THE LAST CHORD.

353.

353-A.

GOOD TASTE IS DEFINED AS "THE FACULTY OF DISCERNING BEAUTY, PROPORTION, AND SYMMETRY" SOME SEEM TO HAVE IT NATURALLY AND OTHERS HAVE TO DEVELOP IT.

THE ELEMENTS OF GOOD TASTE IN ARRANGING OR COMPOSING SEEM TO BE:

    SIMPLICITY AND CLARITY, BUT WITH ENOUGH SUBTLETY TO BE INTERESTING.
        WHICH AGAIN IS
    UNITY AND VARIETY
        IN RHYTHMIC CONTENT
        IN MELODIC CONTENT
        IN FORM, LENGTH, CLIMAX
        IN STYLE OF ORCHESTRATION
        IN STYLE OF HARMONY, CHORD CHOICE
        IN STYLE OF VOICINGS, PROGRESSION
        TENSION AND RELAXATION

WE MAY FIND VARIETY THROUGH:

CONTRAST OF 1) COLOR (ORCHESTRATION)
    ENSEMBLE ALL THE WAY THROUGH WOULD GIVE YOU UNITY BUT NO VARIETY.

    IF THE FIRST 16 BARS ARE ONE COLOR (IE: ENSEMBLE) MAKE THE NEXT 8 BARS A DIFFERENT COLOR (IE: SAXES OR PIANO OR ETC.)

    ALSO CONTRAST A SOLO (OR UNISON) OF ONE COLOR WITH A BACKGROUND OF ANOTHER COLOR.
    (IE: TRUMPET SOLO WITH SAX BACKGROUND)

2) REGISTER
    IF 1ST CHORUS IS VOICED IN LOW REGISTER, PUT 2ND CHORUS IN A HIGHER REGISTER. (IE: TROMBONES 1ST CHORUS AND THEN ENSEMBLE, OR PIANO, OR CLARINET 2ND CHORUS)

    ALSO CONTRAST HIGH SOLO WITH LOW BACKGROUND.
    (IE: HIGH TRUMPET SOLO WITH LOW SAX BACKGROUND)
    (LOW SAXES OR TROMBONES WITH HIGH TRUMPET FIGURES)

CONTRAST IN 3) DYNAMICS
    LOUD AGAINST SOFT.
    IF YOU HAVE BEEN USING A LOT OF LOUD ENSEMBLE DROP DOWN TO A SOFTER SOUND.

    THICK AGAINST THIN ORCHESTRA.
    IF YOU DROP DOWN TO A THIN ORCHESTRA JUST BEFORE YOU BUILD YOUR CLIMAX, THE CLIMAX WILL SOUND MUCH BIGGER.
    ALSO A SMALL BAND WITHIN THE LARGE
    (A PROGRESSIVE, OR DIXIE, OR SMALL COMBO IN THE MIDST OF A BIG BAND ARRANGEMENT WILL GIVE YOU GOOD CONTRAST)
    SPREAD HARMONY CONTRASTED WITH TIGHT (BLOCK) HARMONY.

CONTRAST IN 4) STYLES
    CONTRAPUNTAL AGAINST MELODY AND ACCOMPANIMENT
    CONTRAPUNTAL AGAINST BLOCK OR SPREAD CHORDS.
    PROGRESSIVE AGAINST LEGITIMATE (EXTREME)
    TWO BEAT AGAINST FOUR BEAT.
    RHUMBA VS. FOUR BEAT
    BEGUINE VS FOUR BEAT
    SMOOTH AGAINST SWING
    NO VIBRATO AGAINST VIBRATO
    ETC., ETC.,

DEVIATION FROM THE EXPECTED:

A) RHYTHM
    BY UNEXPECTED ACCENTS
    BY OUT OF METER PHRASES
    BY UNEXPECTED ENTRANCES

B) MELODY
    NOTICE THAT WHEN WE START A SCALE LINE THE LISTENER EXPECTS IT TO CONTINUE. GOOD TASTE DICTATES THAT WE MUST VARY THE SCALE LINE TO HOLD THE LISTENERS INTEREST.
    IE: EX. 355 IS MORE INTERESTING THAN EX. 354 BECAUSE OF THE DEVIATION FROM THE EXPECTED SCALE LINE. THE SAME HOLDS TRUE OF A MELODY THAT STARTS TO FOLLOW A COMMON CHORD LINE.

354. (SCALE)

355. (DEVIATION)

C) HARMONY
    BY SUBSTITUTE CHORDS (PLEASE USE SPARINGLY)
    BY DECEPTIVE CADENCES (SURPRISE CHORDS)

D) FORM (SAME AS RHYTHM)

E) ORCHESTRATION
    IE: IF WE EXPECT A BRASS FILL IN AT A CERTAIN PLACE BECAUSE IT HAS HAPPENED TWO OR THREE TIMES PREVIOUSLY WE MAY FOOL THE LISTENER BY HAVING ANOTHER COLOR PLAY IT. (MAYBE A TIN WHISTLE)

F) DYNAMICS
   SUDDEN SOFT OR SUDDEN LOUD PASSAGES
   UNEXPECTED ACCENTS

WE LIKE TO BE TEASED OR FOOLED A LITTLE BIT, BUT NOT TOO MUCH.

EXTREME DEVIATIONS FROM THE EXPECTED CREATE COMEDY.

EVERY WORK OF ART, WHETHER IT IS A PAINTING, A POEM, A STORY, OR A BUILDING, OR AN ARRANGEMENT, SHOULD HAVE THE QUALITY OF SIMPLICITY!! MAKE YOUR ARRANGEMENT EFFECTIVE BUT SIMPLE.

MOST EVERY WORK OF ART IS BUILT FROM TWO CONTRASTING IDEAS. A MOVEMENT FROM A SYMPHONY OR A POP TUNE IS BUILT FROM TWO CONTRASTING THEMES. NATURALLY THE BIGGER THE FORM, THE MORE CONTRAST IS ALLOWABLE BETWEEN THE TWO THEMES.

IN MOST COMPOSITIONS ALL THE THEMES ARE FROM ONE GERM; EVEN A WHOLE SYMPHONY, 4 MOVEMENTS, SHOULD BE BUILT FROM ONE MAIN THEMATIC IDEA. EXAMPLES 356 TO 386 SHOW SOME OF THE POSSIBLE WAYS TO EXPLOIT A THEME. ONE POSSIBILITY IS BUILDING YOUR SUBORDINATE THEME FROM YOUR MAIN THEME BY TURNING IT UPSIDE DOWN, FREE INVERSION, (YOU CAN CHANGE THE INTERVALS) AND TRANSFORMING THE RHYTHM OF THE MELODY. IN THIS WAY YOU CAN HAVE A SUBORDINATE THEME THAT CONTRASTS (AS MUCH AS YOU DESIRE) WITH YOUR MAIN THEME; AND YET IT IS EVOLVED FROM THE ONE IDEA, WHICH MAKES FOR STRUCTURAL CONSISTENCY.

UNITY VERSUS VARIETY IS ANOTHER PRINCIPLE APPLIED ALL THROUGH ART.
UNITY IS OBTAINED BY A SAMENESS THROUGHOUT (CONSISTENCY)
VARIETY IS OBTAINED BY CONTRAST AND DEVIATION FROM THE EXPECTED.

IN A POP TUNE THE FIRST MELODY AND THE RETURN TO IT AT THE END OF THE CHORUS GIVES US UNITY. THE BRIDGE, (OR SECONDARY THEME) GIVES US THE NECESSARY VARIETY. TOO MUCH UNITY CREATES MONOTONY. (THIS IS SOMETIMES EFFECTIVE IF DONE OBVIOUSLY)

IN YOUR WRITING USE ENOUGH UNITY TO MAKE EVERYTHING SOUND LIKE A PART OF THE WHOLE PICTURE. BUT USE ENOUGH VARIETY TO SUSTAIN THE INTEREST OF THE LISTENERS AND THE PERFORMERS.

JUST WHEN THE LISTENER THINKS HE KNOWS WHAT IS GOING TO HAPPEN NEXT, FOOL HIM BY DEVIATING FROM THE EXPECTED.
IE: IF THERE ARE THREE PHRASES IN A ROW THAT ARE THE SAME (REPETITION OR SEQUENCE) THE LISTENER HEARS THE FIRST TWO AND EXPECTS THE THIRD TO BE THE SAME. THAT IS WHY IT IS IN GOOD TASTE TO VARY IT THE THIRD TIME. (UNLESS YOU WANT MONOTONY)

ALSO NEVER DO ANYTHING OUTSTANDING JUST ONCE IN YOUR ARRANGEMENT (THIS IS VARIETY WITHOUT UNITY) ANY IDEA THAT ATTRACTS ATTENTION BUT JUST OCCURS ONCE, DOESN'T SEEM TO BELONG, BUT IF IT IS REFERRED TO POSSIBLY THREE TIMES THEN IT IS A PART OF A WHOLE PICTURE.
IE: A BIG BLOTCH OF RED IN A PAINTING OF ALL COLORS THAT ARE UNRELATED TO IT, IS OUT OF PLACE. BUT IF THERE ARE OTHER DASHES OF RED ELSEWHERE IN THE PAINTING THEN IT IS A PART OF THE WHOLE. A STARTLING IDEA JUST ONCE IS LIKE A CHARACTER IN YOUR STORY THAT HAS NOTHING TO DO WITH THE PLOT.

WE MODIFY OR BREAK THE RULES (WE HAVE BEEN TAUGHT) FOR VARIETY, BUT WE BREAK THEM ALWAYS OBVIOUSLY AND FORCEFULLY; NEVER TIMIDLY OR HALFWAY.

CONSISTENCY OF TENSION WILL GIVE US UNITY BUT IF EVERY CHORD HAS THE SAME AMOUNT OF DISSONANCE, WE GET MONOTONY. AT THE OTHER EXTREME, IF A TRIAD OCCURS IN THE MIDST OF EXTREMELY DISSONANT CHORDS, WE HAVE A RIDICULOUS AMOUNT OF VARIETY AND NOT ENOUGH CONSISTENCY (UNITY).

THE AMOUNT OF VARIETY AND UNITY YOU USE IS UP TO THE TASTE OF EACH INDIVIDUAL. THIS IS WHAT GIVES EACH ARRANGER INDIVIDUALITY. NO TWO THEMES OR SONGS ASK FOR THE SAME TREATMENT, AND NO TWO ARRANGERS WILL GIVE ANY ONE SONG THE SAME TREATMENT.

SEE PAGE 101 FOR WAYS OF USING VARIETY AND UNITY.

EXPLOITING A THEME OR MOTIVE:
IN A LEGITIMATE COMPOSITION, OR IN A MOVIE, OR RADIO DRAMA, OR TV DRAMA PROGRAM WE OFTEN HAVE A GOOD OPPORTUNITY TO EXPLOIT A THEME. FOLLOWING ARE SOME OF THE DEVICES COMMONLY USED. JUST ONE OR TWO EXAMPLES OF EACH ARE GIVEN HERE. THE AMOUNT OF POSSIBLE WAYS IS STAGGERING.

356.
ORIGINAL THEME

357.
AUGMENTATION

358.
DIMINUTION

359.
DIATONIC INVERSION

360.
GEOMETRIC INVERSION

361.
FREE INVERSION

362.
RETROGRADE (BACKWARDS)

363.
RETROGRADE INVERSION
(UPSIDE DOWN & BACKWARDS)

364.
DIFFERENT RHYTHMS

365.
DIFFERENT RHYTHMS
(ALSO TRY 9/8, 5/4, ETC.,
FAST, SLOW)

366.
CONTRAPUNTAL
(4 VOICE)

367
CONTRAPUNTAL
(2 VOICE)
(IMITATIONS)

368.
CONTRAPUNTAL
(4 VOICE)
(STRETTO)

369
CONTRAPUNTAL
(BASIC RHYTHM OF   )
(TRY TRIPLETS, 16TH NOTES,
ETC.,)

370.
CONTRPUNTAL HARMONY
(CHORDS ARE THE RESULT OF
LINES)

371.
ATONAL COUNTERPOINT
(TONE ROW)

372.
ATONAL COUNTERPOINT
(4 VOICE)

373.
CHORALE STYLE

374.
CLUSTERS
(BUILT FROM INTERVALS
OF MELODY)

375.
HARMONICALLY
(OVER DIFFERENT CHORDS)

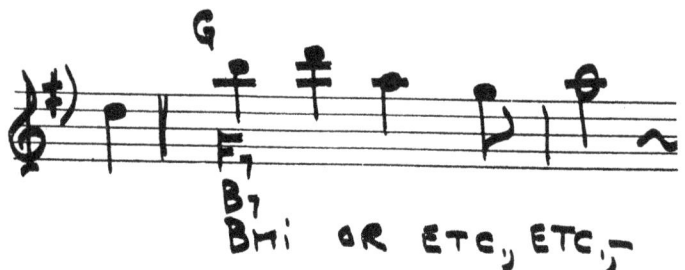

376.
PARALLELS

377.
PARALLELS

378.
MELODY & ACCOMP.

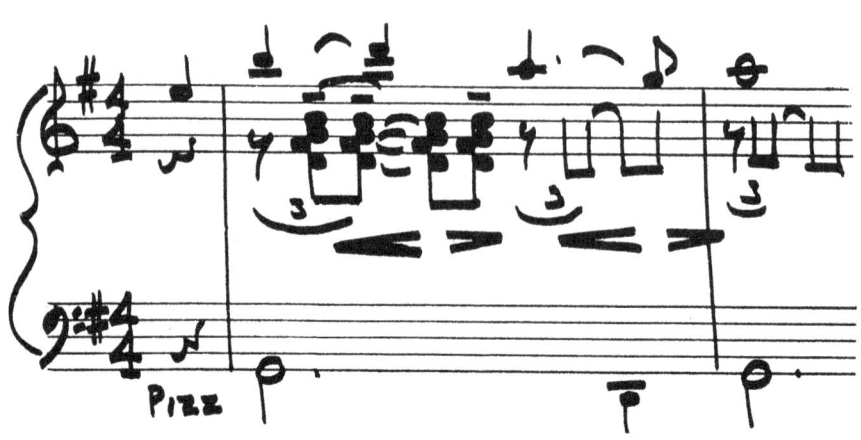

379.
MELODY & ACCOMP.

380.
DIFFERENT ORCHESTRATION
(COLORS, EFFECTS)
(SEE EX. 183 TO 209)

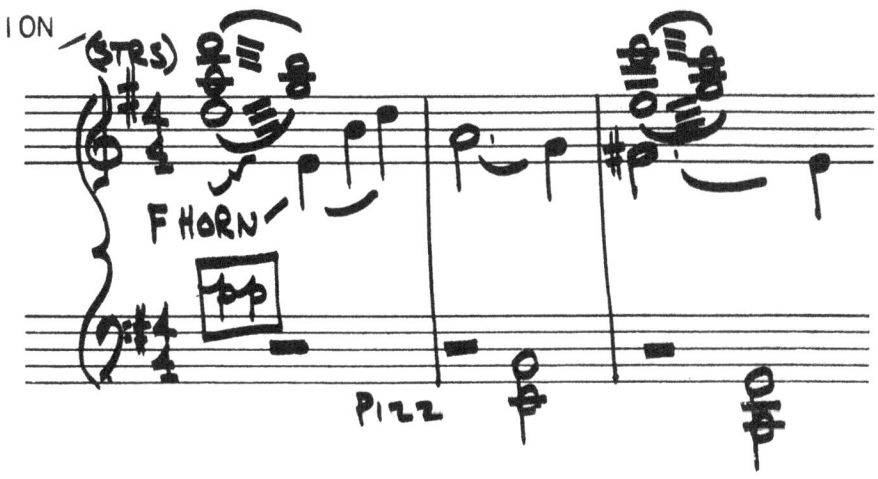

381.
ACCOMPANIMENT OUT OF
FRAGMENT, (WITH NEW
MELODY ADDED)

DIFFERENT MOODS

382.
LOVE THEME

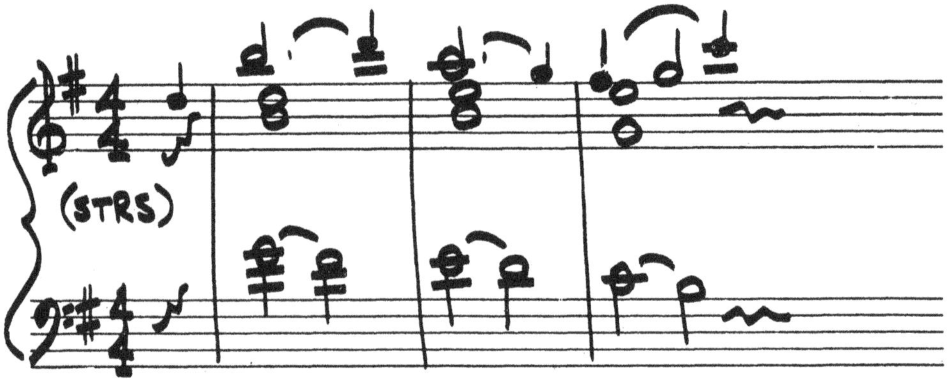

383.
COMEDY

384.
DRAMA

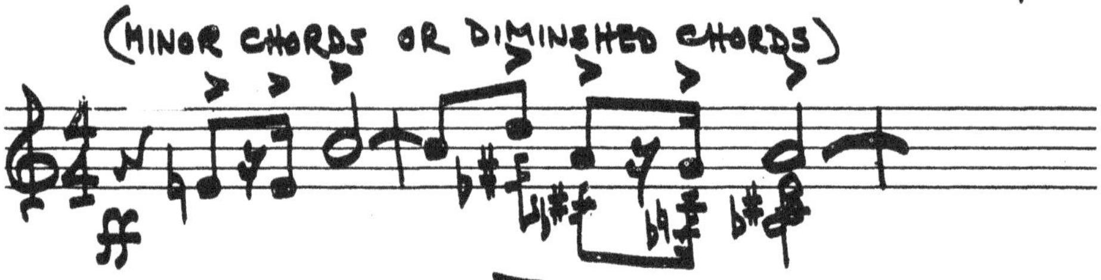

385.
PATHOS OR TRAGEDY

TRY FRAGMENT AS A GROUND BASS
TRY DIFFERENT REGISTERS
TRY SEQUENCES (SEE EX. 343-344)

386.
GRANDEUR

THE SAME THEME MAY BE WRITTEN IN THE STYLE OF
1) A MARCH
2) A DANCE
3) A PASTORAL (EX.325)
4) ANY COMPOSER
5) ANY COUNTRY
6) ANY BAND OR ORCHESTRA
7) ANY COMPOSITION

NOTICE THAT IMITATIONS, OR INVERSIONS, OR RETROGRADES, OR RETROGRADE INVERSIONS, MAY BE ON DIFFERENT LEVELS (STARTING ON ANY NOTE) NOTICE ALSO THAT THEY MAY BE:

1) DIATONIC - (CONFORMING TO THE SCALE OR KEY) EX.359.

2) SYMMETRIC - (EXACT INTERVALS, WHICH USUALLY CARRIES YOU INTO FRESH NEW KEYS) EX. 360.

3) FREE   - (THE CURVE AND RHYTHM IS THE SAME BUT THE INTERVALS ARE LARGER OR SMALLER THAN THE ORIGINAL) EX. 361.

PERMUTATION MEANS CHANGING THE ORDER OF THE NOTES IN YOUR THEME.

RHYTHMIC TRANSFORMATIONS ARE USUALLY NECESSARY TO MAKE INVERSIONS, RETROGRADES, AND RETROGRADE INVERSIONS, SOUND GRACEFUL.

NEVER USE THESE DEVICES MECHANICALLY. SING EVERYTHING YOU WRITE AND IF IT DOESN'T SOUND LIKE AN INSPIRED MELODY, THROW IT OUT OR REHASH IT. WRITING MUSIC MUST BE 75% KNOW-HOW AND 75% INSPIRATION.

RETROGRADE, RETROGRADE INVERSION, AND PERMUTATION ARE ONLY PRACTICAL WITH A VERY SHORT THEME OR MOTIVE.

ECONOMY OF MEANS:

ALL OF THE DEVICES SHOWN IN EXAMPLES 356 TO 386 WILL HELP YOU TO BUILD MORE OUT OF LESS MATERIAL. IT SEEMS TO BE A LAW OF NATURE THAT THE MOST EFFICIENT WAY TO DO ANYTHING IS WITH THE LEAST AMOUNT OF ENERGY.

IN EX. 387, NOTICE THAT THE MELODY IS BUILT OUT OF TWO SMALL FRAGMENTS. ANALYZE THE POP TUNE "DON'T BLAME ME," NOTICE THAT THE MELODY OF THE FIRST SIXTEEN BARS IS ALL BUILT FROM FRAGMENTS OF THE FIRST FOUR NOTES.

IN EX. 387 THE IMPORTANT INNER LINES ARE BUILT FROM FRAGMENTS OF
THE MELODY. USING THE DEVICES FROM EXAMPLES 356 TO 386, A DANCE
BAND ARRANGEMENT COULD BE BUILT THAT IS STRUCTURALLY VERY SOUND.
(IE: THE FILLS COULD BE BUILT FROM FRAGMENTS OF THE MELODY INVERTED
AND TRANSFORMED RHYTHMICALLY, ETC.)   REMEMBER THAT ALL FOUR MOVEMENTS
OF THE GREAT SYMPHONIES ARE USUALLY FROM ONE KERNEL OR CELL THAT IS
STATED NEAR THE BEGINNING OF THE FIRST MOVEMENT.

ANALYZE A SYMPHONY AND FIND HOW THE MAIN THEMES AND SUBORDINATE THEMES
OF EVERY MOVEMENT ARE RELATED.

387.   ALL THE LINES IN THIS EXAMPLE ARE DERIVED
             FROM THE FIRST BAR AND A HALF OF THE FIRST
             VIOLIN PART.

SETUP OF SCORE:
        WOODWINDS OR SAXES AT THE TOP
        HORNS AND BRASS NEXT
        PERCUSSION NEXT   (DRUMS, TIMPANI, XYLOPHONE, CHIMES, BELLS,
                              ETC., PIANO, HARP, CELESTE, ETC.,)
        VOICES NEXT   (SINGING OR NARRATION)
        STRINGS AT THE BOTTOM

ORCHESTRA AND MICROPHONE SETUP

IF YOU WRITE CLEAN, TRANSPARENT ORCHESTRATION, USING MOSTLY PURE COLORS, AND AS FEW MIKES AS POSSIBLE, YOU WILL GET A GOOD BALANCE ON A RECORDING (OR ON THE AIR) I HAVE HEARD SYMPHONY ORCHESTRAS RECORDED BEAUTIFULLY ON JUST TWO MIKES. YOU CAN SET UP THE ORCHESTRA TO GET A GOOD BALANCE INSTEAD OF DEPENDING ON THE MIXER TO BALANCE IT. IF IT SOUNDS BALANCED TO A PERSON SITTING OUT IN FRONT OF THE ORCHESTRA, WHY WOULDN'T IT SOUND THE SAME TO A MICROPHONE OUT IN FRONT?

MY FAVORITE SETUP IS:

388.

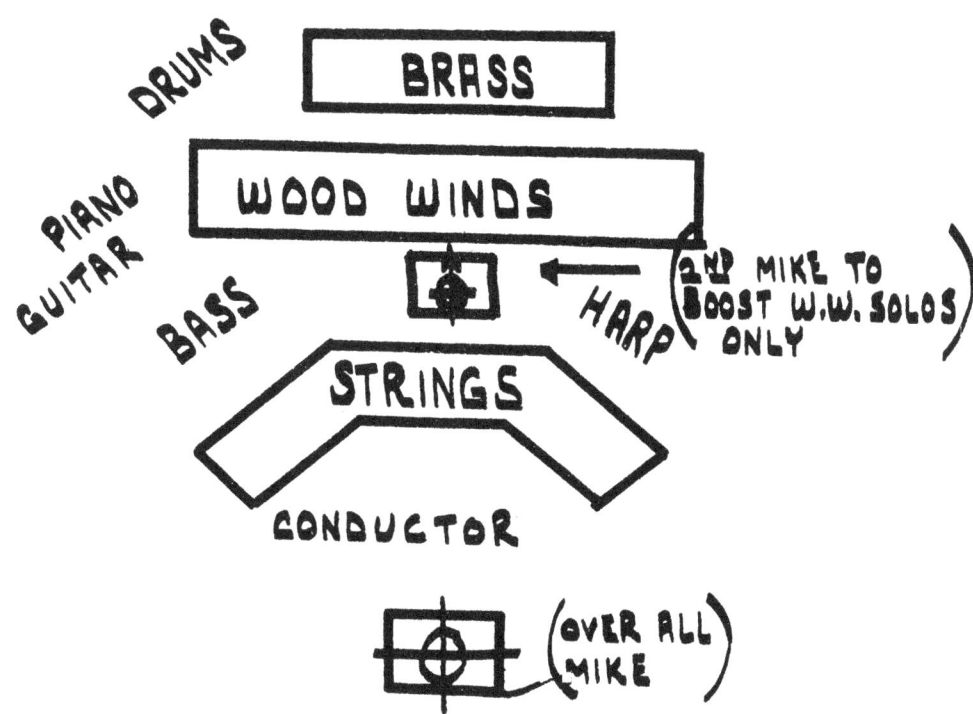

OCCASIONALLY FOR SPECIAL EFFECTS, ADDITIONAL MIKES MAY BE NECESSARY.

ANOTHER SATISFACTORY SETUP IS TO SPLIT THE STRINGS (THOUGH THIS GIVES THE MIXER A LITTLE MORE OPPORTUNITY TO UNBALANCE YOUR ORCHESTRA)

389.

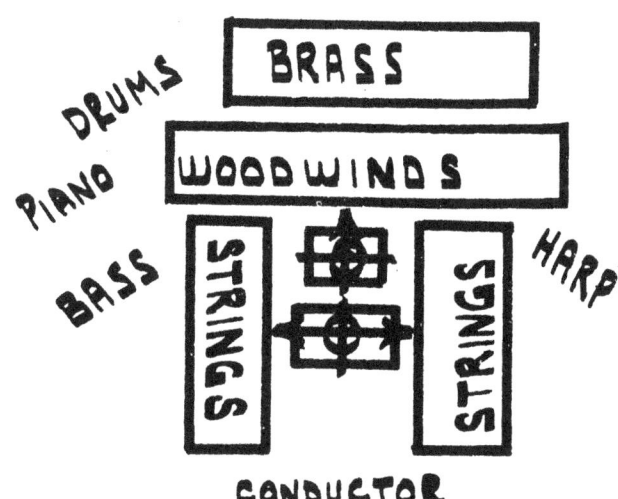

ARTIFICIAL ECHO CAN BE USED VERY EFFECTIVELY AT TIMES.
ALSO IF YOU HAVE A DEPENDABLE MIXER, YOU CAN USE BOARD FADES OR BOARD SNEAKS, IN WHICH THE MIXER GRADUALLY FADES THE ORCHESTRA OUT.

DISTANCE OF INSTRUMENT FROM THE MIKE IS ALSO AN IMPORTANT FACTOR. WHEN YOU LISTEN TO A RECORDING IN WHICH THE MIKE IS RIGHT CLOSE TO AN INSTRUMENT, IT GIVES YOU THE FEELING THAT THE INSTRUMENT IS RIGHT IN YOUR FACE. WITH VOCALISTS SOMETIMES THIS "INTIMATE PRESENCE" IS EFFECTIVE.

IN THE TWO SETUP EX. 388 & 389, NOTICE THAT THE BRASS (BEING THE LOUDEST) ARE THE FURTHEST AWAY FROM THE MIKES, AND THE STRINGS ARE THE CLOSEST. THIS IS GOOD LOGIC BUT CAN BE OVERDONE. IF THE BRASS ARE TOO FAR AWAY, THEY MAY SOUND LATE ON ENTRANCES, OR THEY MAY SOUND LIKE THEY ARE IN ANOTHER ROOM.

NOTICE IN EX. 390, THE SECOND VIOLIN IS TWICE AS FAR FROM THE MIKE AS THE FIRST VIOLIN. IN EX. 391, THE MIKE IS FARTHER AWAY, AND THE SECOND VIOLINS ARE ONLY ONE AND 1/4 TIMES AS FAR AS THE FIRST VIOLINS. ALSO IN EX. 391, THE OUTSIDE CHAIRS ARE IN THE RANGE OF THE DIRECTIONAL MIKE.

390.   391.

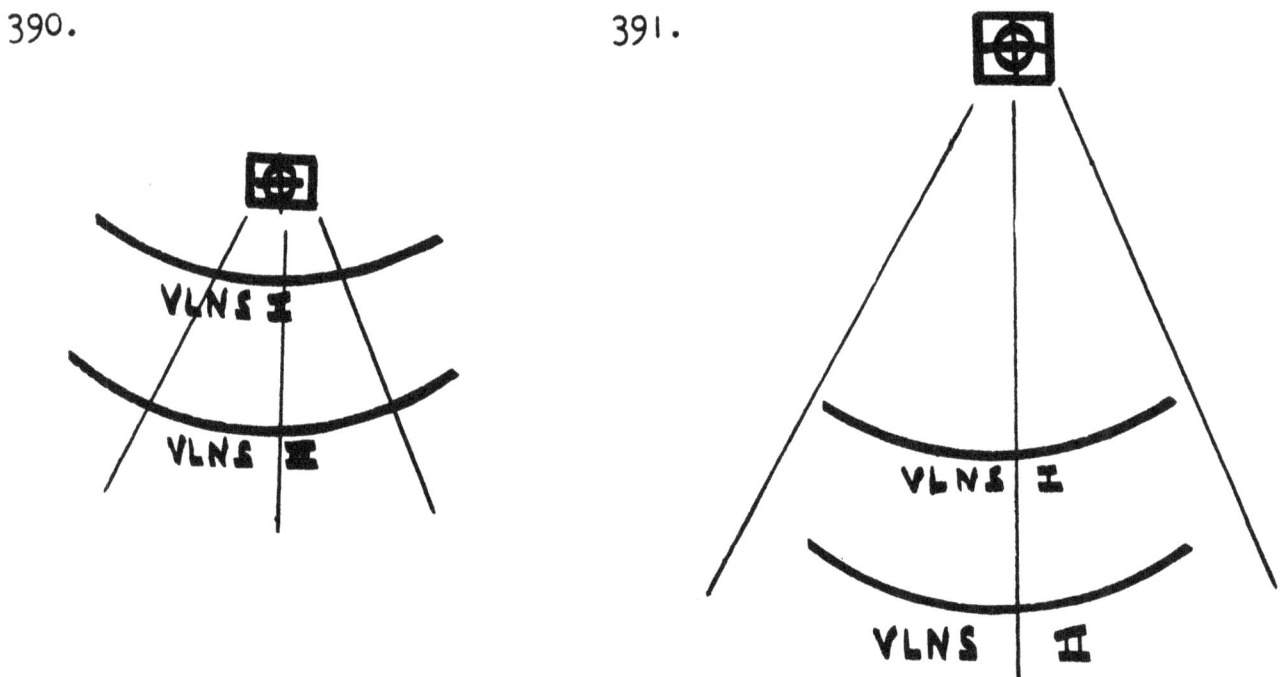

ALSO, DON'T LET THE MIXER BRING OUT THE IMPORTANT LEAD LINE AND DROWN EVERYTHING ELSE IN THE ARRANGEMENT.
THE CLEANER THE ORCHESTRATION AND THE FEWER THE MIKES THE LESS THERE IS TO WORRY ABOUT.
DON'T USE MIKES TOO CLOSE OR TOO FAR AWAY FROM INSTRUMENTS EXCEPT FOR SPECIAL EFFECT.

AFTER YOU HAVE WRITTEN A COMPOSITION OR ARRANGEMENT, CHECK IT FOR:

1) BALANCE OF UNITY AND VARIETY

2) IS IT BUILT FROM JUST A FEW IDEAS, SIMPLE BUT EFFECTIVE?

3) IS THE FORM (PLAN) BALANCED AND CLEAR CUT?

4) DOES THE CLIMAX OCCUR IN A LOGICAL PLACE? (MORE THAN 1/2 WAY THROUGH)

5) IS HARMONY (ROOT PROGRESSION) LOGICAL?

6) IS ORCHESTRATION SIMPLE AND CLEAR CUT?

7) DO ALL YOUR FIGURES SOUND GOOD AT THE TEMPO IT WILL BE PLAYED?

8) IS IT IN ONE MOOD OR STYLE? (CONSISTENCY)

9) ARE ALL PARTS MARKED CAREFULLY? (TEMPOS, DYNAMICS, EXPRESSION MARKS, BOWINGS, BREATHINGS, INSTRUCTIONS, ETC.)

10) SING THROUGH EACH INSTRUMENT PART ON SCORE. DOES EACH PART MAKE SENSE BY ITSELF (ESPECIALLY RHYTHMIC SENSE)

11) WHEN ONE INSTRUMENT OR SECTION DROPS OUT AND ANOTHER SECTION OR INSTRUMENT ENTERS, DID YOU OVERLAP THEM FOR SMOOTH CONTINUITY?

IF THE ANSWER TO ALL THESE QUESTIONS ISN'T YES, YOU'D BETTER DO SOMETHING ABOUT IT.

NEVER BE COMPLETELY SATISFIED. ANALYZE YOUR OWN SCORES AS WELL AS OTHERS. NEVER STOP LEARNING.
STUDY SCORES AND LISTEN TO MUSIC AND ANALYZE:
1) RHYTHM
2) MELODIC LINE
3) HARMONIC STRUCTURE
   A- PROGRESSION   B- VOICING, ETC.
4) ORCHESTRATION (COLORS)
5) FORM (PLAN)
6) STYLE OR MOOD

GOOD LUCK AND I HOPE THIS BOOK HAS HELPED YOU WRITE BETTER MUSIC.

Russell Garcia

NOTES FROM LECTURE, "MUSIC AS A PROFESSION"

SOME OF THE DIFFERENT TYPES OF JOBS IN MUSIC:
- ARRANGING OR COMPOSING FOR
    - DANCE BAND
    - RADIO
    - TELEVISION
    - MOVIES
    - RECORDS
    - PUBLISHERS
        - STOCK ORCHESTRATION
        - LEAD SHEETS
        - PIANO PARTS
    - SINGERS
    - VODVIL ACTS
    - VOCAL GROUPS
- PLAYING AN INSTRUMENT
- SONG WRITING
- SPECIAL MATERIAL WRITING
- SINGING
- CONDUCTING
- BAND LEADER
- COPYIST - LIBRARIAN
- TEACHING
- COACHING (VOCALISTS)
- REHEARSAL PIANO (FOR SINGERS, DANCERS, ETC.)
- MIXER (ENGINEER)
- SONG PLUGGER
- PIANO TUNER
- SELLING RECORDS, SHEET MUSIC, OR PIANOS
- MUSIC CRITIC

IF YOU TRY ALL OF THESE AND FAIL, YOU CAN ALWAYS BUY A MONKEY AND AN ORGAN.

BUT IF YOU HAVE A STRONG DESIRE TO WRITE MUSIC AND HAVE A GOOD POTENTIAL CREATIVE ABILITY, (WHICH EVERYONE HAS IN VARYING DEGREES), PLUS A GOOD SENSE OF RHYTHM, GOOD PITCH PERCEPTION, AND A FAIR MUSICAL MEMORY, PLUS A MIND THAT LIKES TO PUT THINGS IN ORDER, AND ENOUGH DRIVE TO STICK WITH IT, AND SOME ABILITY TO CONCENTRATE;
YOU CAN MAKE YOURSELF A WONDERFUL LIFE IN MUSIC.

CREATING GIVES YOU A JOY AND A SATISFACTION THAT SOME PEOPLE NEVER KNOW.

TO DO ANYTHING GREAT IN ANY ART, I BELIEVE THAT YOUR MOTIVES SHOULD BE TO IMPROVE YOUR OWN MIND AND CREATIVE POWERS AS MUCH AS POSSIBLE (BY STUDYING THE ADVANCEMENT OF THE ART UP TO THE PRESENT TIME, AND THEN TRYING TO IMPROVE ON WHAT HAS GONE BEFORE) SO THAT YOU MAY HELP THE ART IN GENERAL AND ALSO MAKE THIS LIFE A MORE PLEASANT PLACE FOR HUMANITY. THIS LEADS TO THE PROGRESS OF CULTURE AND HUMANITY AND ALSO TO PERSONAL HAPPINESS.

ADVICE:
1) BECOME ADEPT ON SOME MUSICAL INSTRUMENT
2) LEARN TO WRITE EVERY STYLE (DANCE AND LEGITIMATE)
3) STUDY PHILOSOPHY, SEMANTICS, ETC., ETC.,
4) HAVE AN OUTDOOR HOBBY (GOLF, SWIMMING)
5) SET YOUR GOAL AND WORK TOWARD IT EVERY DAY.

A SUGGESTED COURSE OF STUDY FOR THE SERIOUS STUDENT.

1) STUDY HARMONY AND COUNTERPOINT TOGETHER.

    HARMONY TO BECOME FAMILIAR WITH THE CHORDS IN A KEY
    (AND THEIR RELATIONSHIP TO EACH OTHER)
    VOICE LEADING
    ALTERED CHORDS
    MODULATION
    BE ABLE TO WRITE A CHORALE
    SYMMETRIC HARMONY
    WANDERING HARMONY
    COUNTRAPUNTAL HARMONY

    COUNTERPOINT WILL EVENTUALLY TAKE CARE OF YOUR ORCHESTRATION
        COMPOSITION, ETC.

        1ST, 2ND, 3RD, 4TH SPECIES.
        FREE COUNTERPOINT
        WRITE SEVERAL TWO VOICE INVENTIONS (MOTIVE DEVELOPMENTS)
        ORCHESTRATE ONE OF YOUR INVENTIONS FOR STRING QUARTET
        WRITE (ONE OR TWO) THREE VOICE INVENTIONS FOR 3 INSTRUMENTS
        WRITE A CHORUS OF A POP BALLAD FOR 4 OR 5 STRINGS
            UNACCOMPANIED USING CONTRAPUNTAL LINES.
        WRITE A FUGUE. ORCHESTRATE IT.

2) ORCHESTRATION

    MEMORIZE RANGES AND TRANSPOSITIONS AND BEST USAGES OF
        ALL INSTRUMENTS. (MEMORIZE FORSYTHE'S, "ORCHESTRATION")
    ORCHESTRATE A FEW PIANO PIECES
    BE ABLE TO WRITE A DANCE BAND ARRANGEMENT OF ANY STYLE.

3) COMPOSITION

FORM
PLUS ORCHESTRATION

        WRITE AN ORIGINAL 3 PART SONG FORM FOR STRING QUARTET
        WRITE AN ORIGINAL 1ST RONDO FORM FOR STRING QUARTET
            PLUS FLUTE OR HORN OR CLARINET USING TRANSITIONS,
            RETRANSITIONS, EXTENSIONS, INTRODUCTION AND ENDING.
        WRITE A SMALL SONATA ALLEGRO FORM (EX. 392 & 393)

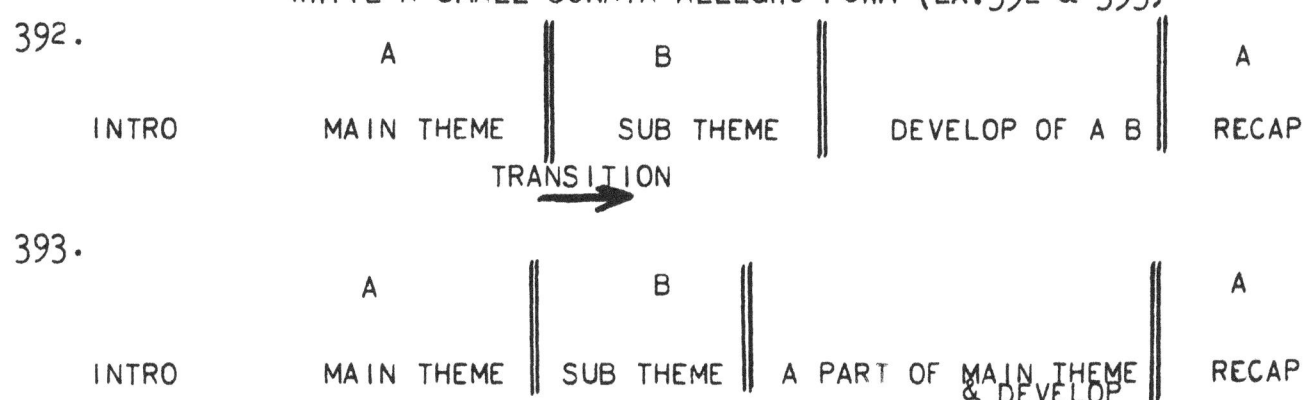

392.

| INTRO | A
MAIN THEME | B
SUB THEME | DEVELOP OF A B | A
RECAP |

TRANSITION →

393.

| INTRO | A
MAIN THEME | B
SUB THEME | A PART OF MAIN THEME & DEVELOP | A
RECAP |

TRANSITION →   RETRANSITION →

STUDY, ANALYZE AND KNOW THE OTHER RONDO FORMS
THE LARGER SONATA ALLEGRO FORMS (IN CONTEMPORARY WORK THE
    TREND IS TOWARD BREVITY. THAT IS WHY THE SHORTER FORMS
    ARE STRESSED HERE)
WRITE A COMPOSITION ON A GROUND BASS
WRITE A PASSACAGLIA
WRITE A CHACCONE
WRITE A THEME AND VARIATIONS (SIMPLE)
WRITE A THEME AND VARIATIONS FOR ORCHESTRA (FREE)

LEARN:
  LEARN TO COMPOSE BY WRITING RHYTHMIC CURVES
  ANALYZE THE STYLE (MELODY, HARMONY, ORCHESTRATION, FORM) AND
      BE ABLE TO WRITE IN THE STYLE OF YOUR FAVORITE COMPOSERS
      OF EACH ERA AND EACH COUNTRY.
  LEARN TO WRITE IN "12 TONE TECHNIQUE"
  WRITE A PRODUCTION ARRANGEMENT FOR LARGE ORCHESTRA(STRINGS, BRASS,
      WOOD WIND, PERCUSSION) ON SOME STANDARD TUNE.
  WRITE A SYMPHONY, A STRING QUARTET, AND A WIND QUINTET

THIS COURSE OF STUDY SHOULD NATURALLY BE MODIFIED TO MEET THE NEEDS,
AIMS, DESIRES AND TALENTS OF EACH STUDENT. ANYONE WHO HAS GONE
THROUGH THE ABOVE SHOULD BE READY FOR ANY TYPE OF COMPOSING OR
ARRANGING WORK.